Anonymous

The Little London Directory of 1677

The oldest printed list of the merchants and bankers of London. Reprinted from the exceedingly rare original; with an introduction pointing out some of the most eminent merchants of the period

Anonymous

The Little London Directory of 1677
The oldest printed list of the merchants and bankers of London. Reprinted from the exceedingly rare original; with an introduction pointing out some of the most eminent merchants of the period

ISBN/EAN: 9783337251543

Printed in Europe, USA, Canada, Australia, Japan

Cover: Foto ©Thomas Meinert / pixelio.de

More available books at www.hansebooks.com

THE LITTLE LONDON DIRECTORY

OF 1677.

THE LITTLE LONDON DIRECTORY

OF 1677.

THE OLDEST PRINTED LIST OF THE MERCHANTS AND BANKERS OF LONDON.

REPRINTED FROM THE EXCEEDINGLY RARE ORIGINAL;
WITH AN INTRODUCTION POINTING OUT
SOME OF THE MOST EMINENT
MERCHANTS OF THE
PERIOD.

LONDON:
JOHN CAMDEN HOTTEN,
PICCADILY.
1863.

INTRODUCTION.

THIS little book might easily, by a competent pen, be made the text to a volume, as large, if not as useful, as the huge "Post Office Directory," of which it was the modest precursor. No such ambitious object as the production of a volume of that class is to be here indulged in. On the contrary, the purpose of the present short introduction is to offer a few suggestions upon topics obviously belonging to the contents of this commercial record of the merchants and *goldsmiths* of London in the second half of the seventeenth century. It will be found to demonstrate the value of not a few family *names* as significant elements of the history of social progress.

It has, indeed, been so in all time. From Homer's catalogues down to the knightly nomenclature of the " Roman de la Rose," and other long-breathed poems of the middle ages; from the Battle-abbey Roll of the conqueror's chiefs at Hastings, and from that of King Henry's army at Agincourt to our modern musters, such documents elucidate acceptably the course of military heroism. The conjecture is as ingenious, as it is just, lately made about *Shakespeare's* early life, that the Admiralty books, with their myriad of seamens' names, may give his in some royal ship, and so account for his perfect sea phrases.

The most interesting *manuscript* lists are those of the notabilities present at the Preston Guild for more than 500 years; and that of the founders of a Library in Hereford 200 years ago. The Guild is in existence still. The books given to the library by Viscount Scudamore, and some hundreds of the county people, were rotting on a damp floor not long since. It may be hoped they are now better cared for.

INTRODUCTION. vii

Equally attractive are the lists still preserved of the zealous contributors to public loans to meet a national crisis. *John Locke* and *Somers* were among the first proprietors of the Bank of England. Those of the East India Company, or the like Stocks were the leading Tories.

The founders of our early colonies—holders of even five-shilling shares—have thus their enduring record; and a diligent collector may enrich his library of tracts with the printed names of all the graduates of old Harvard College in New England in the seventeenth century—so zealously did the Puritans ground their sons in learning.

The present production, although of more moderate pretensions, contains individual names of some historical weight. Its most striking feature is the severance of "*Goldsmiths that keep Running cashes*"—precursors of the modern bankers—from the mass of merchants of London, in 1677.

Before that year the goldsmiths had really been bankers, and proper laws had long been advocated for their better establishment in the craft. This list fixes their residence chiefly in our ancient Lombard Street. Of fifty-eight, the whole number of them, thirty-eight lived there. Of the rest, we have Blanchard and *Child*, partners, in Fleet Street, at the Marygold; and James *Hore* in Cheapside, at the Golden Bottle, for then every house of business had its sign.

Other banking names are striking, viz. the Cornish Bolitho, the Lancashire Hornby, the Yorkshire Duncomb. These men may be presumed to have enriched their descendants who are still conspicuous among us. The rest of the Goldsmiths of 1677 seem to have been little remarkable in the next generation, when, after the revolution of 1688, joint-stock banking, and safe facilities in paper currency took the start which constitutes an era in finance. The capitalists of London in the reign of Charles II. were sorely damaged by his iniquitous shutting of the Exchequer against their legitimate claims. They were content at last to be simply the first holders of stock in the national debt, into which their claims were turned. But Michael Godfrey, the first deputy-governor of the bank, and Sir N.

Herne, afterwards zealous supporters of the new system of banking after 1694, are here only simple merchants. Two other names of the Goldsmiths, James Fowles and James Heriot, deserve special mention. They were Scots; and the Fowles appear to have been long settled in London in connection with their countrymen. In 1695, the Lord Provost of Edinburgh was to address his letters on the subject of Darien to William Paterson at the house of one of the name; and it is no idle speculation to suppose that this goldsmith (a rising banker) of 1677 afforded Paterson, then a pedlar, or incipient merchant, the benefit of his financial experience.

James Heriot has a stronger association with a Scottish worthy of finance, George Heriot, the goldsmith, and the munificent benefactor of Edinburgh, who came south with his patron, King James; and, as his biographer tells us, he prospered here as he had prospered in the north. Besides his bequests to his native town, he left ample legacies to his brothers-german, of whom one was James; and their wealth and name were assuredly represented by the James Heriot the goldsmith of this list.

In it also stands John *Peatterson*, a merchant already, and so giving a body to the tradition in Dumfriesshire which places William Paterson of the Bank of England in the counting-house of a relation of his own name in London about 1677.

The spelling of the two names Fowles and Peatterson is correctly phonetic, so as to show the Scottish nationality of the men; and in the latter case showing also the tact with which Eliot Warburton in his "Darien" makes a Scottish friend criticise his clumsy English pronunciation of the word Paterson.

Another name in the general list, that of Alexander Pope of Broad Street, has an even more famous association, as Mr. Camden Hotten shows in his *Adversaria* for July, 1857. The locality was then a charming suburb of gardens; and although the poet Pope, when taken away with his father, the popish merchant, to be educated in Windsor Forest by a priest, may have been too young to know how genial a home he was losing, he need not

INTRODUCTION. xi

have been too vain, as it is feared he was, to revisit in after life the pleasant abode of his earliest years.

Gresham's garden was in Broad Street, with its lectures on music and all science. King Richard's Crosby Hall, and Shoreditch with its unhappy leman of Edward IV, were hard by; whilst Milton's birth-place, his retreat, and his grave were close at hand.

The picturesque character of old London, graced by the sparkling Thames of olden time, is a circumstance not to be forgotten, when we are calling up the memories of any class of its inhabitants.

In 1677 the city was full of fine residences for merchants; and in this list we meet with names of entertainers of wits of the time. Here is *Fountain*, doubtless father to the wealthy knight with whom Dean Swift was familiar, as shown in his letters to Stella. Here, too, is *Kiffen*, the Baptist Alderman whom James II. could neither affright nor seduce, with a less respectable name of the same class, that of William Lob.

Here is *Benjamin Bathurst*, the founder of

the family distinguished on the Bench and in the State, with *Bragg* their connection. Here is a tribe of the *Houblons*, who furnished the Bank of England with its first Governor, Sir John; and whose names, seven in number, may be read in documents recorded at the Board of Trade claiming convoys for their fleets. These seven names are found in the more interesting record—the sermon of Bishop Burnet at the funeral of this *Houblon*—with his eulogy and city descent from Henry the VIIIth's time. The *Vansittarts* will find their wealthy forefather here, and many more Dutch members of the old church of their nation in Austin Friars. The *Van Milderts* of this list were doubtless progenitors of the learned late Bishop of Durham of that name; and the predominance of Dutch over Flemish merchants settled in London is to be attributed to the ultra-Protestant feeling of that time. Puckle the wit, and the eager projector, is here in the persons of his father and uncle. Nor are the Barnardistons, Ducanes, the Fredericks, Beckfords, and Papillons, Burdetts, Batemans, Biddulphs, Bulteels, Carbonnels, Coventrys, the Dominiques, Crisps, Furleys, and the Holfords, to be omitted.

The "*Richard Steele*" in the list must have been related to Sir Richard, who was more successful in the advocacy of the rights of trade with his pen than in his multifarious commercial schemes.

The special occupations of these merchants are not stated with much precision. After the Goldsmiths come the Black-well Hall factors, representing our ancient staple in woollens, whose privileges were the occasion of a great legal controversy shortly before the date of this little publication; and they were settled with prodigious learning in the Common Pleas by Chief Justice Sir Orlando Bridgman, as may be seen in his logical judgments. One particular address is very interesting. It is at "*the Insurance Office*," then a new institution among us, and only extended with great success in the beginning of the next century, in the reign of Queen Anne.

The Royal Exchange was a prominent place of business for our merchants of 1677. The Dutch walk, the Turkey walk, the *Irish* walk, the Spanish walk, and the like, have a significance far beyond the agreeable cosmopolitan sentiments expressed in the Spectator upon Addison's and Sir Richard Steele's visit to the Exchange of their day, crowded with men from every clime. In these several walks could be found, in the earlier years of the reign of Charles II, the collected members of our various trades beyond sea; and it was from them that the Lord Mayor was directed by a royal order in Council, to have elected the body that was to assist ministers in the preparation of our laws of trade and the colonies. That original order in council, signed by Lords Clarendon and Southampton, is preserved in the City library in Guildhall. It contains an article of extreme interest at this moment, specially providing for the election of the *Italian* merchants to that body. This commercial tie with *United* Italy cannot fail to be strengthened so as to revive an alliance with us too long interrupted by religious prejudice on both sides. The list has a few Italian names, but more Portuguese—perhaps brought over from the connection with "*the*

Royal Houſe of Liſbon" in the perſon of Charles the Second's Queen, received by us with becoming good humour, according to the pungent epigram which bade "*the De'il take Hyde and the Biſhop beſide, that made her bone of his bone.*"

The diviſion of the merchants in their reſpective dignities is worth a paſſing reflection. Some are knights and baronets; ſome are aldermen; the maſs are plain John or Thomas, with a conſiderable ſprinkling of *Miſters*—the maſter of olden times being an addition of worſhip. The Captains and Majors of the liſt were doubtleſs the officers of the trainbands, of no little hiſtoric fame in London, from King John and Magna Carta even to John Gilpin.

The homes of many of the merchants named in this liſt were in the ſuburbs of London, and there they ſeem to have tranſacted their buſineſs, not in the City. We find them at Highgate, ſo well known before as the reſidence of the philoſophic Earl of Arundel, where Lord Bacon died,—at Newington Green, Iſlington, Clerkenwell Green, Hackney, Hogsden, Bethnall Green, Kingsland, Moorfields, Spital-fields, and Mile End Green,—places now so many centres of crowded population, not the sweet rural retreats, which we are content to go for farther a-field, being, like our fathers, fully awake to the delights of forest life.

The *Hogsden* of the list (our Hoxton) is shown to have been pretty full of merchants; and we know how delightful a group of gardens that suburb possessed in the olden time. Not very long after 1677, its worthy horticulturist Fairchild there practised his art with eminent success; and not only founded the annual sermon still preached by distinguished divines every year upon the bounty of the Creator in the gifts of nature, but tried hard with his pen to teach the citizens to adorn London with gardens. This is a consideration well worth pursuing at this moment of London's revival. Her seventy graveyards, so long festering charnel-houses, may, under wise direction, become centres of floral beauty and instructive recreation to our youthful London population.

INTRODUCTION. xvii

Some refided on "The Bridge," the London Bridge for ages covered with dwellings, from one of which the daughter of a rich citizen fell into the Thames to be faved by the bold apprentice Ofborne, who married her, and founded the ducal family of Leeds.

The painted *portraits* of the more diftinguifhed of thefe fathers of our trade would deferve a fpecial ftudy. Sir John Houblon's may be feen at the Bank of England; Benjamin Bathurft's is affuredly pioufly preferved by his ennobled family; Sir John Tulfe, who has left his name perpetuated on the picturefque hill near the Cryftal Palace, muft have poffeffed good tafte enough to be a portrait-painter's patron; and the letter in the Spectator afferting our fuperior appreciation of that branch of art is well juftified in the numerous portraits fcattered all over the land. Our commerce is indeed exceedingly rich in materials of hiftorical portraiture, and in its products. Without oftentatioufly boafting of a fuperiority which is not to be pretended over the ftatefmen who grace fo many halls, our merchants, from the pencils of Holbein and Antonio More down to the latest dates, may challenge comparison with them. The City and its halls are full of them; and Sir Thomas Gresham's design of an university in London could not be better revived and realized than by annexing a fine gallery of merchants' portraits to its other branches of instruction. It ia a good suggestion, that the profit got by the Treasury from the sale of his estate in Broad Street to a Banking Company, should be pursued to its legitimate issue,—the establishment of that university.

The topic of Gresham's University has some elucidation from the list of 1677. Comparatively few merchants then resided in Broad Street, or in Bishopsgate Street. Rents were therefore low in that quarter. In 1760, when the Gresham property was sold, under an Act of Parliament, for the Excise Office, its income was less than 450*l.* a-year; and the government made it up to 500*l.* The sale, however, to the Gresham Chambers' Company, a few years since, netted a very large sum to the Treasury. That surplus is believed to revert to the trusts of Sir T. Gresham's will, since the Acts which have alienated the estate first from the Charity, and then from the Crown, are mere parliamentary titles—quite secure to the occupiers of the land, but not destructive of the rights of the objects of a founder. The matter is indeed under serious scrutiny before the Charity Commission; and it has special claims to the fair consideration of Her Majesty's prime minister.

The *John Temple* of this list was probably of Lord Palmerston's lineage. The Palmers of the list, too, doubtless belonged to the family which almost monopolises the Mercers' Company—Gresham's trustees; and so Sir Roundell Palmer, the Solicitor-General, must not desert his duty. Nor will he have forgotten his own labour of love in Gresham's lecture-room, when he helped his relative, Professor Palmer, to do justice to his charge.

Earl Russell will not, on this occasion, refuse his powerful aid to the improvement of the citizens of London, so often the defenders of liberty, and the advocates of science. The City has indefeasible claims upon Earl Russell's sympathies—if for nothing more—for the sad sacrifice of his great relative Lord William, led, from his prison in the Tower, through the heart of the city to his scaffold in Lincoln's-Inn-Fields, in order to crush the spirit of a people deeply attached to the house of Bedford.

Finally, the Chancellor of the Exchequer, Mr. Gladstone, will readily part with the large proceeds of the Gresham Charity-estate, which, by all the calls of conscience, and the kindred rules of equity, belong to an object which he, of all men, the most approves—the liberal instruction of our youth.

The Harveys of the list are of a honoured stock. They are near kinsmen to Dr. William Harvey, famous in medical history as the discoverer of the circulation of the blood. He passed many of the last years of his eventful life with his brother Eliab, the merchant of London, who possessed " noble seats, and at least 3000*l.* a year," says Aubrey. In those days the physicians, with their College in Warwick Lane, may be held to have been citizens. It was at the Royal Exchange that Drs. Mead and Ratcliffe fought their well-known duel.

INTRODUCTION.

Three original copies of the list of 1677 are known. One is in the Bodleian library; one in the Manchester Free Library, bought for 5*l*., (from this, owing to the kindness of R. W. Smiles, Esq., the Librarian, the present reprint has been made); one was sold at the sale of the Rev. Mr. Hunter's library for 9*l*., although imperfect.

The volume—here reproduced as almost a fac-simile—is a curious little precursor of the London Directory, grown from its first edition of 1732 in 300 pages, to the huge volume, the Post Office Directory of the present day.

In the Lambeth Library there is such a list in manuscript of thirty years earlier date. It is a list of all the inhabitants of London liable to pay tithes, with the amounts due from each.

During the progress of this little volume through the press a most interesting fact relative to the history of trade has come to light. It appears from an old pamphlet that an "*Office of Addresses*" was started as early as 1650, by HENRY ROBINSON, a well known writer on matters of commerce and finance during the commonwealth period. The ideas of this worthy are so advanced and found that it is more than probable that Sir William Petty, who soon after began to write upon these subjects, was indebted to him for some of his liberal views with regard to the extension of trade. Henry Robinson's "Office in Threadneedle Street, over against the Castle Tavern, close to the Old Exchange in London," comes out with a business-like precision in the very advertisement, that promises well for his work—the keeping *particular registers of all manner of addresses*. Then follows a catalogue of subjects of inquiry, so copious and so curious as to be a new proof that there is almost nothing new under the sun! *Sixpence* was the fee, and for this small sum answers to all sorts of questions connected with business could be obtained. The whereabouts of merchants, the arrivals or departures of ships, the current price of certain commodities, were all to be ascertained by visiting this ancient Inquiry Office—the crude off-shoot of a commerce struggling to develope itself, and answering for a time the purposes of a broker's office, the Stock-Exchange, and the modern newspaper teeming with trade advertisements.

Licenſed Octob. 11. 1677.

Roger L'estrange.

A COLLECTION

OF THE

NAMES

OF THE

MERCHANTS

Living in and about

The City of LONDON;

Very Usefull and Necessary.

Carefully Collected for the Benefit of all Dealers that shall have occasion with any of them; Directing them at the first sight of their name, to the place of their abode.

LONDON, Printed for *Sam. Lee*, and are to be sold at his Shop in *Lumbard-street*, near *Popes-head-Alley:* And *Dan. Major* at the *Flying Horse* in *Fleetstret.* 1677.

Preface.

To the Merchants and Traders of the City of London.

Gentlemen,

Lthough the publishing of the ensuing Pamphlet (or Catalogue) may at the first view, seem to several persons a ridiculous and preposterous attempt, yet the Author of this poor Collection humbly hopes, that it will not be exploded or rejected by you, for whose ease and conveniency (together with your forein correspondents) he principally intended it: And if it prove so succesful as to receive a favourable acceptance from your hands, the censure of all other persons not concerned in the conveniency arising by it, will not discourage the Author to proceed

The Preface.

and make such Improvements of this small *Embrio*, as may soon bring it to a perfect birth. He humbly hopes no Apology will be required for such Errata's or Escapes as have been committed as to the Orthography, or true writing of the respective Names of this Catalogue, as well for that he hath found it a very difficult thing, to procure so ample an Account of Names as he hath done; as also in regard his main design is, to publish this forthwith, to the end that if those persons who are concerned in the Use of it, do give it a favourable Receptance, he may set forth an Additional Catalogue far more correct and accurate; wherein if he may receive Encouragement accordingly, he shall not in any thing be better satisfied than that his poor Endeavours shall have answered those Ends for which they were intended.

Advertisement.

Hereas, *since the enſuing Tract was in the Preſs, the Author hath diſcovered the Habitations of ſeveral other Merchants, not comprehended in the Alphabetical Order; he hath therefore thought fit (rather than to omit them) to inſert them in the laſt Page of this Book by themſelves. And whereas the Author intends ſhortly to Reprint this Catalogue, with additions; he doth therefore deſire, that for the better furtherance of the next Edition, all Merchants, as well ſuch as ſhall be newly arrived from beyond the Seas, as alſo all ſuch as ſhall be newly ſet up, would be pleaſed to give in their Names and Habitations to* Samuel Lee *Stationer, over againſt the Church, near* Popes-head Alley *in* Lombard Street. *And if it happen that any Omiſ-*

Advertisement.

Omission shall be made of any Merchants Names in this or the ensuing Edition, let the parties concerned repair to the said Mr. Lee, *where they may probably receive satisfaction. And if any Bill of Exchange happen to be drawn upon any Tradesmen or Shopkeepers under the denomination of Merchants, if they repair to the place aforesaid they may receive due Information.*

A COLLECTION
OF THE
MERCHANTS
Living in and about
the CITY of *LONDON*.

[*A.*]

Robert Abbot, *Bow-Churchyard.*
Allen Ackworth, *Burchin-Lane.*
Edward Addams, *Great St. Bartholomews.*
John Addis, *Bednal-Green* or at the *Sun* in *Lumbard-Street.*
Elias Adrian *and Company* in *Broad-street.*
Thomas Allcock, in *Grubstreet.*
Richard Aley, *Mincin-Lane.*

[*A.*]

Richard Aley *Devonshire-house.*
Cornelius Alderwerldt, *Freemans-yard, Cornhill.*
Mr. Allen, *Cateaton-street Blackwell Hall Factor.*
Edward Allen, *Towerhill.*
Daniel Allen, *Fanchurch-street.*
William Allen, *Princes-street.*
Edward Allen *Queen-street, removed into Tower-street.*
Mr. Allen, *Mugwell-street.*
Mr. Allen *Spittle-fields.*
Mr. Almand Clement's Lane, Church-Alley.
Samuel Alstone, *Basinghall-street, Blackwelhall Factor.*
Russel Alsope, *Lau. Pount. Lane.*
Isaac Alvarez, *in St. Mary Ax.*
Jacob Jesrum Alvarez, *in St. Mary Ax neer Bury-street.*
Herbert Allwyn *Shipyard Woodstreet.*
Thom. & Peter } Andrews, *Crutchet-Fryars.*
Alderm. Andrews, *Walbrook.*

William

[*A.*]

William	Andrews,	*Fanchurch-Street.*
Mr.	Andrado	*Leadenhall-street.*
John	Archer	*Mark-lane.*
George	Archer	*Cheapside.*
Iohn	Archer	*Gravel-lane Houndsditch.*
Jeremiah	Armiger	*Houndsditch.*
Capt.	Armstrong,	*Newington-Butts.*
John	Arthur	*Austin-Fryars.*
Daniel	Arthur	*Broadstreet.*
Henry	Ashurst Senior,	*Watling street.*
Henry	Ashurst Junior,	*St. Johns-Street.*
Mr.	Ashur	*Aldermanberry.*
Mr.	Ashlier	*Newington Town.*
John	Ashby	*Friday-street.*
Alderm.	Aske	*Love-lane Aldermanberry.*
Francis	Ashty,	*Minories.*
Thom. & John	Atterberry,	*Angel-Court Throgmorton-Street.*
William	Attwood	*Queen-Street.*

[*B.*]

William   Attwood *Newington Town.*
Daniel   Axtell *to be spoken withal at the Sign of the Purse in Loathbury.*
Sir Benj. Ayloffe *Fanchurch-street.*

[*B.*]

Joseph & William } Bateman *Martins lane.*
Edw.   Baker *New Court Throgmorton Street.*
Richard Baker *Poultrey.*
John   Baker *Aldermary Church-yard.*
Mr.   Ballard *St. Dunstans-hill.*
Jacob   Baldwyn *Still-yard Thames-Street.*

Peter

[B.]

Peter	Baldwyn *Mark-lane*.
Mr.	Balts *Crown-court Spittle-Fields*.
John	Banks, *Fanchurch-street*.
Rich.	Banks *Gravel-lane Houndsditch*.
Mr.	Banishford *Hatton-garden*.
Peter	Barr *Austin-fryars*.
Will.	Barron *Throgmorton-street*.
Edw. & Hen. }	Barkley *Throgmorton-street*.
Edw.	Barton *Angel-Court Throgmorton-street*.
Rich.	Barker *New-Court Throgmorton-street*.
Sir Sam.	Barnadiston *Bishopsgate within*.
Arthur	Barnadiston *Hogsdon, to be spoken with at Mr. Hedges in Broadstreet*.
Pallatia	Barnadiston *Hummerton in Hackney*.
Natha.	Barnadiston *Hackney*.
Thom.	Barnadiston *Hackney-Town*.

[B.]

Mr.	Barnadifton, *Well-Street Hackney.*
Arthur	Barron *Coleman-ftreet.*
George	Barron *Garlick-hill.*
Mr.	Barrot *Budge-row.*
John	Barrot *Pickle-Herring.*
John	Barrot *Execution Dock.*
George	Barnes *Love-lane.*
Gerard	Berens *Mincin-*lane.
Mr.	Bard *Old Bethelem.*
John	Barcklet *Fanchurch-ftreet.*
Thom.	Barker *Seething-lane.*
Mr.	Bafsford *Kings-Arms-yard Coleman-ftreet.*
Mr.	Baffet *Bankfide.*
Richard	Baffe *Trinity-lane.*
William	Battalie *Mark-lane.*
Mr.	Battle *Broadftreet.*
John	Batthurft *Cornhill.*
Benjam.	Batthurft *St. Mary Ax.*
Cap. Th.	Battfon *Stepney near the Church.*
Ezeck.	Batchelor *without Aldgate.*
Thom.	Bawdes *Berry-ftreet.*
William	Baxter *Fanchurch-ftreet.*

Simon

[*B.*]

Simon	Baxter *Highgate,* to be spoken withal in *Bush-lane* at a *Packers.*
Richard	Baxter *Vine-Court Spittle-fields.*
William	Bayly, *Shadwel.*
William	Beard, *Lawrence Pountney's Lane.*
Simon	Berringer, *Threadneedle street.*
Phillip	Beaumont, *Dukes-place.*
Charl.	Beavor *Michael-lane.*
Edw.	Beaker, *Ironmonger-lane.*
Mr.	Beavor, *Crooked-lane.*
Will.	Beakon, *Catcaton-street.*
Edw.	Beakon, *George-yard Lombard-street.*
Mr.	Beavor, *Goodman's-fields.*
John	Beare, *Crutchet-fryars.*
Hump.	Beane, *Turkey-walk Excha.*
Mr.	Bearns, *Mincin-lane.*
Isaac	Bean, *Bow-lane.*
Thom.	Beacon, *Minories Haiden-Yard.*
Rich.	Beavoir, *Pelmell.*

[*B.*]

Will. Beck, *Crutchet-fryars.*
Thom. Beckford, *Thames-ſtreet.*
Abrah. Beak, *St. Dunſtans-hill.*
Richard Beckford *Tower-ſtreet.*
Samuel Beak, *Buttolph-lane.*
Mr. Bedkins, *Bank-ſide.*
Edward Bell *Crutchet-fryars.*
Thom. Bell, *Tower-hill.*
Mr. Bellows, *Philpot-lane.*
William Bellamy, *St. Dunſtans-hill.*
Francis Bellows, *White-chappel.*
Adam Bellamy, *Dice-key.*
John Bedell, *Bloſoms-Inne.*
William Benſon, *Winchester-ſtreet at Mr. Holride.*
William Bennet, *Borough South-wark.*
John Benes, *Beaver-marks.*
Sir John Bendiſh, *York Buildings in the Strand.*
Mr. Berry, *St. Antholings.*
Moſes Berrew, *Dukes-place.*
John Berry, *Philpot-lane.*
Charles Beſt, *Bloomſberry.*

Arthur

[B.]

Arthur	Betsworth, *Bow-lane.*
Mr.	Byfield, *Hackney.*
Mr.	Byfield, *Ditto.*
Thom.	Boyer, *Laurence Pount-lane.*
Mr.	Bible, *Colchester-street.*
Edward	Bickley, *Basinghall-street.*
Sir Theo.	Biddolph, *Austin-fryars.*
Mr.	Biddolph, *Aldermanberry.*
Mr.	Bidford, *Newington Town.*
Edward	Bilton, *Creedchurch-lane.*
William	Bird, *Broadstreet at a Packers.*
Mr.	Bird, *Fishstreet-hill.*
John	Bird, *Martins-lane.*
Mr.	Blackman ; *Ironmonger Lane.*
Thom,	Blackmore, *Kings-street.*
Robert	Blackmore, *at a Barbers Ironmonger-lane.*
Thom.	Blackmore, *Bartholomew Close.*
Mr.	Blacklesly, *Tower-street.*
Thom.	Blashfield, *Bartholomew Close.*

Mr.

[*B.*]

Mr.	Blackstone, *Bishopsgate-Street.*
Mr.	Bland, *Hogsden.*
John	Blewitt, *Great St. Hellens.*
Mr.	Bleatingston, *Distaff-lane.*
John	Blowfield, *Threadneedle Street.*
Sir Tho.	Bloodworth, *Maiden-lane.*
Fred.	Blunkard, *Sice-lane.*
Mr.	Bloonkard, *Sice-lane.*
Robert	Bloone, *Crutchetfryars.*
Benj.	Blundell, *at the house of Mr. John Sheldon in Cannon-street.*
Thom.	Bodley, *Houndsditch, Gun Yard.*
George	Boddington, *Great Saint Hellens.*
Rene.	Bodvin, *Kingstreet.*
Thom.	Boghes, *Loathberry.*
Richard	Bogon, *little St. Hellens.*
Mr.	Boliford, *Bush-lane.*
Mr.	Boldt, *Buttolph-lane.*
Mr.	Boldens, *Bush-lane.*

Andrew

[*B.*]

Andrew	Bonneel, *Mark-lane.*
John	Bonneel, *St. Mary Ax.*
Mr.	Bonset, *Islington.*
Jerim.	Bonneel, *and Compan. Old Jury.*
John	Bon, *New Court Throgmorton-street.*
Mr.	Booby, *St. Mary Ax.*
Thom.	Boon, *Ditto.*
Rich.	Booth, *Princes-street.*
Mr.	Booby, *Broadstreet.*
Edw.	Bovey, *Mark-lane.*
Edw.	Bovery, *St. Mary Ax.*
Joseph	Bowles, *Laurence Pountneys Hill.*
Thom.	Bowhey, *Tokenhouse-yard.*
John	Bowden, *Bush-lane.*
John	Bowles, *Mark-lane.*
William	Bowles, *Mincin-lane.*
Mr.	Bowles, *St. Mary Ax.*
Franc.	Boynton, *Broadstreet.*
Adrian	Beyer, *Lauren. Pountney Lane.*
James	Brace, *Fanchurch-street.*
Mr.	Bragg, *Broadstreet.*

Franc.

[B.]

Franc.	Branetti, *York buildings in the Strand.*
Mr.	Bradley, *Execution Dock.*
Leona.	Bray, *Shoreditch.*
John	Brand, *Cheapside.*
Tho. & John	} Brailsford, *Tokenhouse-yard.*
Mr.	Bradford *Harp-lane.*
Roger	Bradley, *Bishopsgate Street over against the Post-house.*
Mr.	Bray, *Execution Dock.*
Mr.	Brewest, *Great St. Hellens.*
John	Brittin, *St. Mary Ax.*
Robert	Brittin, *Bury-street.*
Mr.	Brittin, *Gray-fryars.*
John	Brinckley, *Princes-street.*
John	Bryant, *and Company Cat-eaton street.*
Rich.	Bryant, *Shad. Thames.*
John	Bridges, *Queen street.*
Mr.	Bridges, *Goodman's fields.*
Nath. Will. Rob.	} Bridges, *Austin-fryars.*

Will.

[B.]

Will.	Brifhead, *Bankfide.*
Mr.	Brown. *Crutchet-fryars.*
Tho.	Brown, *Bury ftreet.*
Edw.	Brown, *and Comp. with* Mr. Adrian, *Broadftreet.*
Mr.	Brown, *Nicholas lane.*
Will.	Brown, *Cannon ftreet.*
Mr.	Brown, *Mile-end Town.*
Benja.	Brownfmith, *Pudding-Lane.*
Edw.	Brown, *Fanchurch ftreet.*
Arnold	Brown, *Mincin lane.*
James	Brown, *Swithings lane,*
Mr.	Brown, *Coleman ftreet.*
Mr,	Brooks, *Bufh Lane.*
Mr.	Brooks, *Bucklerfberry.*
Gerrard	Bruce, *Mincin Lane.*
John	Buckworth, *Crutchet Fryars.*
John	Bucher, *Bankfide.*
Edw.	Buckridge, *Crown Court Broadftreet.*
Mr.	Buinet, *Laurence Poult. hill.*
Mr.	Bulock, *Armitage.*

Sam.

[*B.*]

Sam.	Bultell, *Anstin-fryars.*
John	Bull, *St. Martins lane.*
Capt.	Bonfoy, *Little Tower hill.*
James	Burkin, *Mincin lane.*
John	Burton, *Abchurch lane.*
Franc.	Burnell, *Bush lane.*
John	Bonner, *Petty France.*
Mr.	Burin, *Spittle Fields.*
Bobert	Burdit, *Gravel lane Hounsditch.*
Mr.	Burden, *Colemans Alley.*
Will.	Burd, *Hackney Town to be spoken withal at Mr. Sherwoods, Broadstreet.*
Edw.	Burket, *Bankside.*
Edw.	Burrish, *Gracechurch street.*
J. Bapt.	Burnell, *near the New Exchange in the Strand.*
John	Burnell, *St. Mary hill.*
Abrah.	Bush, *Mark lane.*
John	Bush, *Fanchurch street.*
James	Bush, *Mincin lane.*
Edw.	Bushel, *Little St. Hellens.*
John	Bush, *Ditto.*
Mr.	Burden, *Vine-Court, Spittle Fields.*

Mr.

[*B.*]

Mr.	Buſton, *Roſemary Lane.*
Mr.	Butts, *St. Mary Ax.*
Sir Wil.	Butler, *Pauls Wharf.*
Will.	Butler, *Nicholas Lane Foxes Ordinary.*
Rich. & Tho.	Butler, *Clements Lane.*
Mr.	Butler, *Goodmans Fields.*
Mr.	Butthard, *Broadſtreet.*
Mr.	Butington, *Mun Yard Black Fryars.*

[*C.*] Ed-

[C.]

Edmond	Callender, *in Tower Street.*
Mr.	Calwell *in Colemans Alley.*
Mr.	Camfield *in Great Saint Bartholomews.*
John	Canham *little Saint Hellens.*
Thom.	Canham *Leadenhall street.*
Roger	Capple *Bishopsgate without.*
Matth.	Carleton *Fanchurch street.*
Abra,	Caris, *Mincin Lane.*
Tho.	Carew *Dukes place.*
Tho,	Carew *Tower hill.*
Tho.	Cary *Ditto.*
John	Carlock *Throgmorton street.*
Will.	Cartell *ditto.*
John	Carter *little Tower street.*

Rich.

[C.]

Rich.	Carrel, *Aldermanberry*.
Mr.	Carrel *Auſtin-fryars*.
Joſeph	Carrel *in Throgmorton-ſtreet, or Warwick-Court*.
Joſeph	Carpenter *Budgerow*.
Mr.	Carpenter *Leaden-hall-Street*.
William	Carbonneel *Mark-lane*.
Sir Fra.	Chaplin *Berry ſtreet*.
Rob.	Chaplin, *Saint Swithins Lane*.
John	Chapman *Great St. Hellens*.
John	Chapman *Broad ſtreet*.
Mr.	Chapman *Biſhopſgate without*.
Mr.	Chapman *Baſſinghall-ſtreet, Blackwelhall Factor*.
Mr.	Chadwick *Fanchurch-ſtreet*.
Jam.	Chadwick *Kings Street*.
Mr.	Chalwel *Tower Royal*.

[C.]

Fra.	Chamberlin *La. Poun. lane.*
Cha.	Chamberlin *Great Saint.*
Mr.	Chang *Pauls wharf.*
Rich. & John	Chandler *Aldermanberry.*
Isaac	Chatwood *Hogsden.*
Freder.	Chevecox *Broadstreet.*
Tho.	Cheuely *Oxford Court Canon street.*
Hen. & Mat.	Chitty *Bishopsgate street within.*
John & Rob.	Chomble *Philpot lane.*
Sir Fra.	Clark *little St. Hellens.*
Samuel	Clark *Throgmorton-street.*
Mr.	Clark *Pudding lane.*
Henr.	Clark *Poultrey.*
Mr.	Clark *Law. Poun. lane.*
John	Clark *Hogsden,* at his Warehouse in *Olive-tree Court Leadenhall-street.*
Mr.	Clark *Kingsland.*

Mr.

[C.]

Mr.	Clark *by the Horse-ferry Westminster.*
Edw.	Clark *and Compa. Cheapside.*
Will.	Clark *Barthol. Close.*
Sam.	Clark *Barthol. Close.*
Tho.	Clark *Love-lane.*
Tho.	Claxton *Bishopsgate within neer Thredneedle street.*
Edward	Claxton *Queen street.*
Sam.	Clay, *Law. Poun. lane.*
James	Cleapole *Bush lane Scot yard.*
John	Clemon *Jewen street.*
Mr.	Clenues *Bednal Green.*
Mr.	Clenes *Waping.*
Mich.	Clipsham *Saint Dunstans hill.*
Mr.	Cliff *Bankside.*
Alen	Cliff *Algate.*
Sir Tho.	Clouterbock *at Mr. Clouterbock's house in Threadneedle Street.*
Jasper	Clouterbock *in ditto* Street.

[C.]

Mr. Coats *Pudding-lane.*
Mr. Cofing *Lime-ſtreet.*
Will. Cockram *St. Swithins-lane.*
Mr. Cole *at Mr. Pilkington's, Buſh-lane, Scot-yard.*
George Cole, *Bartholomew-lane, Ship-yard.*
Will. Cole, *Thames-ſtreet.*
Mr. Cole, *Buſh-lane, Scot-yard.*
Mr. Cole, *near the new Poſtern.*
Hen. Collier *Nicholas-lane.*
Mr. Collier *Borough of Southwark.*
Peter Collier *Little Moor-fields near the Gun-Tavern.*
Jam. Collins *Philpot-lane.*
Tho. Collet *Thames-ſtreet.*
John Coleman *Saint-Swithins-lane near Lombard ſtreet.*
Mr. Collier *Aldermanbury, Blackwelhall Factor.*
Thom. Compere *Fiſhſtreet hill.*
David Conyard *Fanchurch-ſtreet.*

Will.

[C.]

Will.	Conen *Laur. Pount. Lane.*
John	Cooker *Crutchet-fryars.*
Thom.	Cooper *Well-Court Soaper-lane.*
Hen.	Cornish *Cateaton-street near Blackwelhall-gate Factor.*
Mr.	Corn *Newington Green.*
Mr.	Cook *Chain Alley.*
Will.	Cook *Mark-lane.*
Mr.	Cook *Fanchurch-street.*
John	Cook *Austin-fryars.*
Ralph	Cook *Laur. Pount. hill.*
Tho. & Joh.	Cook, *Basinghall-street.*
Mr.	Cook *Goodmans-fields.*
Thom.	Cook *Hackney.*
George	Cock *Greenwich.*
Edw.	Cooth *Basinghall-street.*
Peter	Coston *Sherbon-lane.*
Edw.	Coston *St. Dunstan's hill.*
Dan.	Coston *Hackney Town.*
Mr.	Cordial *Bankside.*
Rich.	Cotton *Redriff.*
Adam	Cottrill *Bush-lane Scot-yard.*

[C.]

Tho.	Coulson *Tower Royal.*
Mr.	Coventrey *Threadneele-str.*[sic.]
Walter	Coventrey *Gr. St. Hellens.*
George	Cowart *in Basinghall Street.*
Mr.	Cox *Newington Town.*
Joseph	Cox *Berry Street.*
Benja. & Jam.	Cox, *St. Martins Lane.*
Mr.	Craker, *London-wall.*
Eben.	Craker *Barnaby Street Southwark.*
Tho.	Crawley *Mincin-lane.*
John	Cranenbergh *St. Martins lane.*
Mr.	Christopher *Ironmonger lane.*
Abrah.	Christian *Threadneedle Street.*
Edw.	Crisp *Towerhill.*
John	Crisp *Breadstreet.*
Elias & Mr.	Crisp Lounes *in Cheapside at the Angel near Breadstreet.*
	Will.

[C.]

Will.	Crisp *Cheapside at the Hen and Chickens.*
James	Cropp *Fanchurch Street.*
Jacq.	Crosse *Philpot lane.*
John	Crosse *at the Three Pigeons in Cornhill.*
John	Crose *Lymestreet.*
Mr.	Crosburn *Lovelane.*
Rich.	Crosman *Lovelane.*
John	Croger *Armitage, East-country Walk Exchange.*
Tho.	Croom *Nicholas lane.*
Twi.	Crowder *Lymestreet.*
Tho.	Crowdell *Colemanstreet Bell Alley.*
Mr.	Crow *Queenstreet.*
Will.	Crouch *Berrystreet.*
Mat.	Cadwell *Broadstreet Excise Office.*
Mr.	Cumporter *Barnabystreet.*
Mr.	Cumporter *Berrystreet.*
Mr.	Cutler *Basinghall-street, Blackwelhall Factor.*
Tho.	Cutler *Austinfryars.*

[*C.*]

Tho.	Cutler *Broadstreet.*	
Mr.	Cutteris *Berrystreet.*	
Mr.	Cuttalis *ditto.*	
John	Curtis	Little Trinity-lane.

[*D.*] Tho.

[D.]

Tho. Dade *Suffolk-lane.*
Mat. Daffing *St. Mary Ax.*
Mr. Dakers *Clarkenwell Green.*
Mr. Dallington *Roodlane.*
Henry Dandy *Beerlane.*
Peter Daniel *the Bridge.*
Robert Daniel *neer Alhallows Thames-street.*
Mr. Daniers *Peters-hill.*
Mat. Datheler *St. Mary Ax.*
Tho. Dashwood *Copthall Court Throgmortonstreet,*
Fran. & Sam. } Dashwood *without Bishopsgate.*
Edw. Davenport *Little St. Hellens.*

Mr.

[*D.*]

Mr.	Davenport	*Ironmonger-lane.*
John	Davalwid	*St. Martins-lane.*
Tho.	Davall	*Kings-Arms-Yard Colemanstreet.*
Jacob	David	*Little Tower-street,*
John	Davis	*Aldermanbury Love lane.*
Tho.	Davits	*Moorfields near the Postern by Petty France.*
Tho.	Davis	*Broadstreet.*
Mr.	Dawson	*Lovelane.*
Mr.	Dawes	*Horse Ferry West.*
Nich.	Dawes	*Little Towerstreet.*
Mr.	Dawes	*Roodlane.*
Tho. & Mr.	Death Death	*Marklane.*
Edm.	Deathick	*Copthall Court Throgmortonstreet.*
Tho.	Dean	*Pancrast-lane.*
Rich.	Dean	*Old Gravel-lane.*

David

[D.]

David	Debarri *at Mr. Dorvills Walbrook.*
Peter	Debarr *Broadstreet.*
Mr.	Debarr *ditto.*
John	Debart *St. Martins-lane.*
John	Deboys *Aldermanberry. Love-lane.*
Thom.	Decraw *Colchesterstreet.*
Jacq.	Decocque *Threadneedle-street.*
Ignat.	Decoque *Lymestreet.*
Mr.	Decluse *Islington.*
Alvaro	Decosta *Budgerow.*
Mr.	Decostus *Dukes-place.*
Peter	Decoker *Cullam Street.*
Rowl.	Dee Senior, *Poultry.*
Rowl.	Dee Junior, *Bowlane.*
Sir Ba.	Degomaz *Berrystreet.*
John	Degrave *Bishopsgate without Half-moon Alley or Angel Alley.*
John	Degrave *Old Fishstreet.*
Abrah & Corn	Degelder } *White Chappel, Adam and Eve Court.*

John

[D.]

John	Delachambre *Fanchurch-ſtr.*
Iſaac	Dellèliers *Leadenhall ſtreet.*
Mr.	Deliens *Roodlane.*
Mr.	Delorey *Berry Street.*
Franc.	Deliz *ditto.*
Gabr.	Delaport *Abchurch lane.*
Robert	Deluna *Great Saint Hel-*
Joſ.	Delliviers *Throgmort. ſtreet.*
Lyon	Delliviers *ditto.*
Peter	Delmey *Lymeſtreet.*
Peter	Delmay *Barnabyſtreet.*
John	Delmey *Pancras lane.*
Mr.	Delebarr *Hackney Town.*
Wil.	Delawood *Nicholas lane.*
John	Delowry *Gracechurchſtreet. near Fanchurchſtreet at an Ironmongers.*
Mr.	Delane *Hogſden.*
Mr.	Delacy *Berryſtreet.*
Fra.	Delate *at the hand and Glove in Cannon-ſtreet.*
Mr.	Delate *Cullam-ſtreet.*
Mr.	Demingo *Mugwell ſtreet.*
Mr.	Demancing *Harp lane.*
John	Demanel *ditto.*

Dan.

[D.]

Dan.	Demetrius *Berryſtreet*.
Dan.	Demetrius *Three Crown Court Southwark*.
Solo.	Demodina *Great St. Hel-*
Nath. & James	Denew, *Marklane*.
Benj.	Denew *Shadwell*.
Nath.	Denham *Lymeſtreet*.
Edw.	Denham *Garlick-hill*.
Rich.	Dent *Auſtin-fryars*.
Mr.	Denon *the Poſtern*.
Mr.	Depoſtus *Dukes Place*.
Abrah.	Deporta *St. Mary Ax*.
Anth.	Depremont *Auſtin Fryars*.
Franc.	Depary *Fanchurch-Street*
Mr.	Dermedo *St. Mary Ax*.
Mr.	Deſkin *Pancras-lane*.
Peter	Devitt *Leadenhall-ſtreet*.
Will.	Dewitt *Buſh-lane Scotch-yard*.
Mich.	Dewing *Princeſs Street*.
Will.	Deworth *Lauren. Pountney Lane*.

Mr.

[D.]

Mr.	Dewker *Cullam Street.*
John	Deway *Leadenhall Street.*
Mr.	Dewell *ditto.*
Mr.	Devester *Broadstreet.*
Chris.	Deynot *Cullam Street.*
Mart.	Deynens *at Mr. Webs Throgmorton-Street.*
Mr.	Dickson *Crown-Court Fish-street Hill.*
John	Dickinson *Throgmorton street.*
Benj.	Diens *St. Dunstan's hill.*
Will.	Disher *Walbrook.*
Mr.	Dison *Bankside.*
Lewis	Doe *Aldermary Church-yard.*
Mr.	Dodsworth *Hummerton in Hackney.*
Chris.	Dodsworth *Poultrey.*
John	Doggett *Lawrence Pouut. Hill.*
David	Dooley *Swithin-lane.*
Mr.	Doolenson *Kingsland.*

James

[*D.*]

James — Donalson *Roodlane.*
John — Dorvill *Walbrook.*
Mr. — Dorasalis *Copthal Court, Throgmorton Street.*
Mr. — Dormon *Bell Alley Coleman-street.*
John — Drake *at Mr. Colemans in Swithin lane near Lombard Street.*
Tim. — Drake *Bunhill.*
Sam. — Draper *Tokenhouse-yard.*
John — Dregue *Angel Court without Bishopsgate.*
Phil. — Duboys *Great Trinity lane.*
Thom. — Ducke *Suffolk-lane.*
Paul — Dockminique *Vine Court Spittlefields.*
Pall. — Dockminique Junior, *Coleman-street.*
Peter & Jam. } Ducaine *Pancras-lane.*
Benja. & Sam. } Ducane, *Queenstreet*

Peter

[*D.*]

Peter & Ant. } Dugua, *Covent-garden Henrietta Street.*

And. Duff *Lodger Bishopsgate-street next an Upholsters.*

Henry Dunster *Mincinlane.*
Henry Dunster *Roodlane.*
Mich Dunwell *Colemanstreet.*
Rich Dunidge *and* Comp *Devonshire house.*
Thom. Duncombe *Colemanstreet Blackwelhall Factor.*
Dan. Duprie *Artillary-lane.*
John Durdan *Bankside.*
Dan. Duthais *Aldermary Church, at Mr. Lewis Doe.*
Mr. Dikes *Colemanstreet.*

[*E.*]

John Eaft *Oxford Court Cannon Street.*
Mr. Eaft *Horfey-down.*
Ifaac Eaftwick, *Hackney Town.*
John Eaton, *Buttolph-lane.*
Nich. Eaton *ditto.*
Theod. Ecckelfton, *Gracechurch Street Crown-Court.*
Sir Jam. Edwards *Iflington.*
John Edwards *Philpot-lane.*
Will. Edwards *Coleman-ftreet.*
Dan. Edwards, *Walbrook.*
Palati Edwards, *Mary Old-ftairs Southwark.*
Mr. Edwards, *Ropemakers Alley.*
Hump. Edwin *Great St. Hellens.*
Mr. Edworth *Hogfden.*

[*E.*]

Mr.	Eggleston, *Bankside.*
John	Eglesfield *at the Pewter-platter Cannon-street, Lodger.*
Johnmartin	Elkins, *Law. Poun. lane.*
Mr.	Elkins *Bishopsgate without.*
Matth.	Elison, *Cannon-street near London-stone.*
John	Elison *Berry-street.*
Franc.	Elison *Mark-lane.*
Jerem.	Elwise *Tokenhouse-yard.*
Ald.	Ellis *Saint Pauls Church-yard.*
Mr.	Elson *at the Postern Blackwelhall Factor.*
Rich.	Emes *Fanchurch-street.*
Mr.	Emson, *Warwick Court in Warwick-lane.*
Rich.	Ely, *Bishopsgate-street over against the Posthouse.*
John	Evans *at Mr. Sparows a Packers in Swan Alley Coleman-street.*

John

[*E.*]

John   Evans *Michael-lane.*
John   Eyles *Great St. Hellens.*
Derick   Eyles, *Leadenhall-Street.*
John   Eldreed *at Mr.* Folio *in Dove-Court.*
Mr.   Ahearns. *Law. Pou. hill.*

[*F.*]

Mr. Fade *Bowlane.*
Mr. Jos. Feak *Grace-church-street Nagshead-Court:* (and Comp.)
Sam. Feak *Bow-lane.*
Edw. Fane, *Philpot-lane.*
Mr. Fanne, *Broadstreet.*
Prosper Fenton, *Seething-lane.*
Rob. Fendall, *Nich. lane.*
Rob. Fellowes; *Aldersgate-street.*
John Fellowes, *Throgmorton-street.*
George Finch *Great St. Hellens.*
Tho. Finch, *Ditto.*
Mr. Finch, *Petty France by Moorfields.*
Edw. Fincham, *Budge-row.*
Mr.

[*F.*]

Mr.	Fincham, *Kingsland.*
John	Flavill, *Law. Pount. hill.*
Mr.	Fleming, *St. Mary Ax.*
Mr.	Fletcher, *Thomas Apostle.*
Mr.	Fletcher, *Spittle-fields.*
Mr.	Fleet, *Mark-lane.*
John	Farfax, *Bunhill.*
Tho.	Farington, *his Warehouse, Mincin-lane, at a Packers.*
Tho.	Firming, *Three Kings Court Lombard-street.*
George	Fisher, *ditto.*
Franc.	Flide, *Bankside.*
Mr.	Flide, *Milkstreet.*
Mr.	Folio, *Berrystreet.*
Rich.	Folio, *Broadstreet.*
John	Folio, *ditto.*
Rob.	Folkner, *Lymestreet.*
Jef.	Foldes, *Loathburry.*
James	Foules, *Clements-lane at a Milliners.*
Rich.	Foot, *Roodlane.*
Sir Ri.	Ford, *Tower-hill.*

[*F.*]

Mr.	Ford, *Kings-Arms-yard. Colemanstreet.*
Mr.	Ford, *Shadwell.*
Jer.	Forman, *Law. Pount. hill.*
Mr.	Fortley, *Execution Dock.*
Anth.	Foster, *Berrystreet.*
Rich.	Foster, *Law. Pount. hill.*
Will.	Foster, *Three Kings Court Lombard-street.*
Mr.	Foster, *Queenstreet.*
Mr.	Foster, *at the Ball in Lombard-street.*
Peter	Fountain, *Watling street.*
Mr.	Founds *Pickle-herring.*
Sam.	Foxley, *Nagshead-Court Gracechurch street and Comp.*
Sam.	Fulwood *Throgmorton-street.*
Matth.	Fuller, *Cateaton street.*
John	Furley, *at Mr. Peter Langley Gracechurch-street.*
John	Forley *St. Dunstans hill.*

Tho.

[F.]

Tho.	Framton, *Milkstreet near the Red Cow.*
Jos,	Frances, *Camomile street.*
Mr.	Frances *Clarkenwell.*
Simon	Francia, *Leaden hall street.*
Dom.	Francia, *ditto.*
Sir Jo.	Frederick, *Old Jury.*
Will.	Freeman, *Fanchurchstreet.*
John	Freeman, *ditto.*
Ald.	Freeman, *Deadmans-place.*
Mr.	Frencham, *Leadenhall Street.*
Phil.	French, *Bushlane Scot-yard.*
Basil	Fyerbraste, *Mark-lane.*

[G.]

Hen. Gall, *Great St. Hellens.*
John Gardner, *Fanchurch-street.*
Franc. Gardner, *Bow Church-yard.*
Will. Garfoot, *Nicholas lane.*
Mr. Gaseronne, *St. Mary Ax.*
John Gasp, *Tokenhouse-yard.*
Dan. Gates, *Artichoak-lane Wapping.*
Franc. Gay, *Basinghall-street.*
Mr. Gay, *Hogsden.*
John Genopen, *Castleyard Westminster.*
Hen. Gennen, *at Mr. Dukes Suffolk lane.*
Mr. Gener, *Milkstreet.*

Mr.

[G.]

Mr.	Gewan *Drans Yard Westminster Street.*
Mr.	Gibson, *Waterlane.*
[I]John	Gibson, *at Mr. Preston's Brewhouse in St. Katharines.*
Mr.	Gibness, *Blackfryars.*
Hen.	Gibes, *Clarkenwell.*
Will.	Gibes, *Southwark.*
Thom.	Glover, *Clements lane.*
Thom.	Glover, *Nich. lane.*
Mr.	Goyer, *Princes street.*
Mr.	Goldens, *Austin-fryars.*
Will.	Golstone, *Nich. lane.*
Hen,	Gold, *Brigendine Court, Basinghall-street.*
Sir Th.	Gold *Aldermanberry.*
John	Gold, *Crutchet-fryars in Gold Court.*
Nich,	Gold, *Lymestreet.*
John	Gold, *Turkey Walk in the Exchange, or at Clapham.*
Jam.	Gold, *Islington, Turkey Walk.*

Mr

[G.]

Mr.	Gold, *Newington.*
Cha.	Goldstone, *ditto.*
Mr.	Goldney, *Bloomsbury.*
Sam.	Godfrey, *Poultrey.*
Benj.	Godfrey, *Tokenhouse yard.*
Mr.	Godard, *Mugwell Street.*
Mich.	Godfrey, *Bush-lane.*
Tho.	Goddard, *Coleman street.*
Mr.	Goddard, *Little Britain.*
George	Goderis, *Laurence Pountney lane.*
Edw.	Godwin, *Soaper lane.*
Mr.	Gooding *Bishopsgate without.*
Hen.	Goodhew, *Buttolph lane.*
Anto.	Gommeswares, *Creedchurch lane.*
Anth.	Gomeserd, *Berry street.*
John	Gunston, *at Blackwelhall.*
Jacq.	Gonsaldus, *Dukes Place.*
Ja.	Gonsalus, *Leadenhall Street.*
Christ.	Goore, *Coleman street.*
George	Gospright, *Tokenhouse Yard.*

Will.

[G.]

Will.	Goflin, *Pancras lane.*
Thom.	Gurden, *Turkey Walk at the Exchange.*
John	Gurden, *Mark-lane.*
Mr.	Gouff, *Armitage.*
Mr.	Gandiat *at a Packers, Loathbury.*
Cha.	Gravener *in Watling-ſtreet at the Black-Swan.*
Roger	Gray *Crutchet-fryars.*
Nich.	Gray *Barge yard Crutchet Fryars.*
Roger	Gray, *Garlick Hill.*
Mr.	Granenta, *Lymeſtreet.*
Mr.	Grayſo, *Moorfields.*
John	Grace *Half-Moon Alley Biſhopſgate without.*
Phil.	Graves *Martins lane.*
Anth.	Green, *Biſhopſgate without.*
Mr.	Grindall, *Dukes place.*
Richard	Griffeth, *Biſhopſgate ſtreet.*
Thom.	Griffeth *ditto.*
Edw.	Griffeth *Barge Yard Bucklerſberry.*

Tho.

[G.]

Tho.	Griffeth *at a Packers in Eastcheap.*
Rich.	Griffeth, *Bucklersberry.*
Mr.	Grinwell *Colemanstreet, Blackwelhall Factor.*
Mr.	Groves *Dukes-place.*
Phil.	Grover *Martins-lane.*
John	Grove, *Princes street.*
Antho. Adam, Fred.	} Gronen *Devonshire house.*
Rich.	Gronden, *Old Fish-street.*
Mr.	Gumper *Bunhill.*
Will.	Gun *Billingsgate.*

[*H.*]

Franc. Hacker, *Gun yard Houndsditch.*
Peter Hacker *at Paul Darby, Leadenhall street.*
Mr. Hackwell, *Hackney Town.*
Jasp. Haines, *Thames street.*
Rob. Hagshaw, *White-hart Court.*
John Hagshaw *and Turner, Suffolk Lane.*
Will. Hage, *George Yard Lombard Street.*
Mr. Hall *at the Postern, Blackwelhall Factor.*
Edw. Hall *Gravel lane Houndsditch.*

Mr.

[*H.*]

Mr.	Hall, *Chequer Yard Dowgate.*
Hen.	Hall, *Islington.*
John	Hall, *ditto.*
Mr.	Hall, *Stepney.*
Mr.	Hall, *Berry-street.*
John	Hall, *Fanchurch street at Mr. Baxter.*
Nath.	Hallride, *Winchester street.*
Roger	Haley, *Scot Yard, Bush Lane.*
John	Halworthy, *Swithins-lane near Lombard Street.*
Sir Mat.	Halworthy, *Hackney, Spanish Walk Exchange.*
Edw.	Halford, *Bun Hill.*
Edw.	Halford, *Clarkenwell Green.*
William	Hamley, *Thames Street.*
Mr.	Hamond, *Fanchurch street.*
John	Hamford, *Buttolph lane.*

Chris.

[H.]

Chris.	Hambleton,	*Bush lane, Scot yard.*
Stephen	Hames,	*Bull and Mouth Street.*
Hen.	Hamson,	*ditto.*
Walter	Hampton,	*Gravel lane Houndsditch.*
Mr.	Hamle	*Tooly street.*
Mr.	Hancock,	*St. Laurence lane.*
John	Hanccoufe,	*Berry street.*
Mr.	Hantbotow	*Broadstreet.*
Mr.	Hanwock,	*Budge-row.*
Rob.	Hanson,	*Sice-lane.*
Rich.	Hanson,	*ditto.*
Mr.	Hanes	*Coleman Street Blackwelhall Factor.* [sic.]
Mr.	Hartley,	*Fanchurch-Street.*
Thom.	Hartley,	*Throgmorton street.*
Nath.	Hartley,	*Swithin's lane.*
Ralph	Hardwick,	*Grace-church Street.*

Tho.

[*H.*]

Thom.	Hardwick *Hackney, Spanish Walks.*
Tho.	Hardwick *London Wall near Broadstreet.*
Mr.	Harwick *Loathberry.*
William	Harwell *Colchester street.*
Hen.	Harbin *Mark-lane.*
John	Harbin *Great Saint Hellens.*
Edw.	Harrison *Roodlane.*
John & Will.	Harrison *Clements-lane.*
Hen.	Harris *Saint Dunstans Hill.*
Mr.	Hart *Throgmorton Street.*
Tho.	Hartops *Lymestreet.*
Mr.	Harrow *Winchester street.*
John	Harwood *Mich. lane.*
Mr.	Harwood *St. Antlins.*
John	Harwood *Mile-end Green.*
Mr.	Harwood *Mile-end Town.*
Mr.	Harvey *Swithin's lane.*
Jo.	Harvey *Beerbinder lane.*
Mr.	Harvey *St. Mary Hill.*
Ralph	Hanwock *Waping.*

Will.

[*H.*]

Will.	Harlman *at Mr.* Cha. Corcelus *in Waping.*
Mr.	Hanly at *Fresh-Wharf.*
Anth.	Harrispe, *Coleman-street, King's-Arms-Yard.*
Tho.	Harrington *Mark-lane.*
Hen.	Haswell *Bush-lane.*
John	Haselwood, *Goodmans-fields.*
Mr.	Hasell *at the Spread Eagle in Gracechurch Street.*
John	Hatner *Winchester Street.*
Joseph Hayward and Daniel Wagfield	} in *Butolf-Lane.*
Mr.	Hawes, *Clement's lane.*
Mr.	Hawkins *Colledge Hill.*
Chris.	Hawkins *Walbrook* at Mr. Dishers.
Mr.	Hawkes *Clapton Hackney.*
Claud.	Hayes *Fanchurch Street.*
John	Hayes *Little St. Hellens.*
James and Joseph	} Hayes, *Gracechurch-street.*
Rob.	Hubold *Great St. Hellens.*

[*H.*]

Sir Nat.	Herne *Loathbury.*
Jos.	Herne *at Sir* John Frede- [sic.] ricks *in Old Jury.*
Sam.	Heron *African house.*
Will.	Hedges *Basinghall Street.*
Mr.	Hedges *Broadstreet.*
Mr.	Hemmings *Basinghall Street Blackwel-hall Factor.*
Isaac	Hemming *St. Mary hill.*
Thom.	Heming *Tokenhouse Yard.*
John	Hency, *St. Martins lane.*
Rich.	Hamden *at Daniel Mercer in Bartholomew Lane.*
Mr.	Henman *Bankside.*
Peter & Pierce	Henrique *Walbrook.*
Cha.	Herle *Aldermanberry.*
Peter	Herringhook *Budge-row.*
Mr.	Hermond *Bishopsgate without.*
Charles	Herle *Junior and Comp. in Aldermanberry.*
Will.	Hester *Borough Southwark.*

Mr.

[*H.*]

Mr.	Hester *Bow Churchyard.*
Benj.	Hewling *Coleman street.*
Rob.	Hews *Kingsland.*
William	Hibert *in Bell-Alley, Coleman-street.*
Matth. & Abra.	Heybert, *Nags-head Court, ditto.*
Will. & Jos.	Hide, *Milkstreet, at the Rose.*
Bedingfield	Higham *Seething-lane,*
John	Hill *Crutchet-fryars.*
Mr.	Hill *Broadstreet.*
John	Hill *Leadenhall-street.*
Franc.	Hill *Bucklersberry.*
Edw.	Hill *the Postern.*
John	Hill *Minories.*
Mr.	Hill *Bishopsgate without.*
Mr.	Hill *Shadwell.*
Mr.	Hill *Rredriff.*
Edw.	Hill *Basinghall-street Factor.*
Mr.	Hillet *St. Antlins in Watlin-street.*

[*H.*]

Nath.	Hilton *at Newington, his Warehouse near the Bear and Fountain in Loathbury.*
Joseph	Hincham *Pudding-lane.*
Thom.	Hinchman *Aldersgate Street.*
Nich.	Hinde *Abchurch lane.*
James	Hinde *Bush-lane.*
Mr.	Hinton *ditto.*
Mr.	Hockton *Grubstreet.*
John & Peter	Hoet *Lymestreet.*
Mr.	Holfsted, *at a Packer's in Nicholas's-lane.*
John	Holmes *in Coleman-street.*
Andr.	Holmes *in Nags-head-Court in Clements-lane.*
Nich.	Hollaway, *in* Nicholas's Lane. *And*
Mr.	Collet *in Company.*
Tho.	Holder, *at the African-House.*
Edw.	Holford, *the Hambrough-Walk.* Will.

[*H.*]

Will.	Hodges *Basinghall Street.*
Rich.	Holt, *Bishopsgate street.*
Mr.	Holt *Ironmonger lane.*
Mr.	Holmes *Nicholas-lane.*
Tho.	Holmes *Walbrook.*
John	Holeman *Bell Alley Colemanstreet.*
Will.	Holgate *Alderman-berry.*
James	Holland *Woodstreet.*
Mr.	Holsam, *Jewen street.*
Mr.	Holcomb *Hatton garden.*
Rich.	Holder, *Roodlane.*
Sir Wil.	Hooker *Crown Court Grace-Churchstreet.*
Will.	Hooker *Lymestreet.*
Caleb	Hooke *Pye-Alley Fanchurch Street.*
Mr.	Hooper *Wapping.*
Chris.	Hopkins *Fanchurch street.*
Edw.	Hopegood *Loathbury.*
Mr.	Holte *Hummerton in Hackney.*

Mr.

[*H.*]

Mr.	Howard	*Bow Church-yard.*
Mr.	Howson,	*Aldermanbury.*
Rich.	How	*at Billingsgate every Morning.*
Henry	Hovener	*Swithins Lane.*
Abrah.	Hovener	*Islington.*
Abr. Isaac and Jam. }	Houblon,	*Winchester-Street.*
John	Hoblon	*Threadneedle Street.*
Peter	Houblon	*Burbinder Lane.*
Peter	Houblon	*Sice Lane, Senior and Junior.*
Maj. Pet.	Houblon,	*Budgerow.*
Nich.	Hudson	*Towerhill.*
Abra.	Hudson	*Colchester-street.*
James	Hutton	*in Durham Yard.*
Mr.	Hulford	*Lambeth.*
Henr.	Hunter	*Crutchet-fryars.*
Hen.	Hunter	*Mincin-lane.*
Tho.	Hunt	*Fanchurch-Street.*
Tho.	Hunt	*Bow-lane.*

Tho.

[*H.*]

Tho. *H*oughton, } *Abchurch Lane.*
     and Bereclif
     in Company

David *H*utchingson St. *Mary hill.*

George *H*ockenhull, *Hackney.*

John *H*ough *Gravel lane Hounsditch.*

Ald. Joh. *H*ough *Clarkenwell Green.*

Steph. *H*ouffan, *Thredneedle-street.*

John *H*ousan, *ditto.*

Alexand. *H*osea *in Momford Court in Milk-street.*

[J.]

Will. Jarret *Lime-street.*
Jam. Jackson *Broadstreet.*
John Jackson *Clements-lane.*
Stephen ⎫
Joseph ⎬ Jackson,   *Pye - Alley*
Jems   ⎬   *Fanchurchstreet.*
Robert ⎭
John Jackson *Tokenhouse Yard.*
Phillip Jackson *Lymestreet.*
Mr. Jackson *Fleet-Bridge.*
Stephen Jackson *St. Mary hill.*
James Jacob *Lymestreet.*
Will. Jacom,   *Aldermary Churchyard.*
Abraham Jacob *Hatton garden.*
Theod. Jacobson,   *Still - yard Thames-street.*
Samuel James *Threadneedlestreet.*

Peter

[*I.*]

Peter	James, *St. Mary Hill.*
Samuel	James *Tokenhouse Yard.*
Abraham }	Jaggard neer Billings-
Francis }	gate.
John	Japoney *Bush-lane.*
Mark	Jarvis *Colemanstreet.*
Mr.	Ibrook *Dukes-place.*
Mr.	Jerman *Bankside.*
Sir Rob.	Jeffereys *Lymestreet.*
John	Jeffery *Saint Mary Ax.*
Mr.	Jekell *Wine-Office-Court Fleetstreet.*
Rich.	Jelley *Michael-lane.*
Durr.	Jenkinson, *Broadstreet.*
Rich.	Jenkinson *Coleman-street.*
Widd.	Jennings *Towerstreet.*
John	Jennings *Shadwell.*
John	Jenkins *Hogsden.*
Ald.	Ireton *Finsbury.*
Sir Arth.	Ingram *Hatton-garden.*
Will.	Ingram *Winchester-street.*
John	Johnson *Buttolph-lane at a Coopers.*
Will.	Johnson *Old Gravel Lane.*
Capt.	Johnson *Mile-end-Green.*

William

[I.]

Will.	Jones, *Bankside neer the Wind-mill.*
William	Jones, *St. Mary Ax.*
Peter	Jones, *ditto.*
Roger	Jones, *ditto.*
Henry	Jones *Abchurch lane.*
Leek	Jones *Queen-street.*
John	Jones *Bush-lane.*
John	Jones *Basinghall-street.*
John	Jones *Mincin-lane.*
William	Jordan, *Basinghall street.*
Thomas	Jorden *Billeter-lane.*
Anthony	Jorden *Thames Street Cole harbor.*
Thomas	Jorden *Swedeland Court Tower hill.*
John	Jorden *Pettycoat lane.*
Merel	Jorden *Clements lane.*
Peter	Joy *St. Dunstan's hill.*
Mr.	Joyle *Armitage.*
John	Joliff *Threadneedle-street.*
John	Israel *Armitage.*
John	Ive *Colchester street Tower hill.*
Ald.	Jurin *Throgmorton-street.*
Will.	Joliff *in the Strand.*

William

[J.]

William Johnson *at a Cheesemongers in Thames-street neer Buttolph-lane.*
John Jurin *St. Dunstans hill.*
Isaac Jurin *Great St. Hellens.*
Mr. Jurin *Sice Lane.*
William Justice *Rosemary Lane.*

[K.]

George Kate *Angel Court Bishopsgate without.*
Mr. Kem in *Laurence lane.*
Mr. Kelling *Clements lane.*
Franc. Kemp *Sice Lane.*
John Kent *Basinghall street.*
Thomas Kent *Bankside.*
James Kenier *Michael Lane.*
Henry Kendall *Bishopsgate Street.*
John Kendall *Strand.*
Henry Kendall *Basinghall Street, Blackwelhall Factor.*
John Kenuty *Horsley-Down Southwark.*
Peter Kesterman *Laurence Poun. lane.*

Thomas

[K.]

Thomas Kett *Gravel Lane.*
Mr. Keys *Islington.*
William Kiffin *little Morefields.*
Rich. Kickerbart *in Whitechappel near the Barrs.*
Mr. Kickerine *Watling street.*
Mr. Kitle *Throgmorton street.*
Mr. Kimball *Laurence Pount. hill.*
Lem. Kingdom *Cornhill.*
Edw. King *Lymestreet.*
Mr. King, *Peters Alley.*
Mr. King *Waping.*
Mr. King *Hogsden.*
Mr. King *Bednall Green.*
Isaac Kingsland *in Thames street near the Customhouse.*
John Knape, *Basinghall street.*
Sir Rob. Knightly *Seething Lane.*
Mr. Knightly *Thames street.*
Luce Knightly *Basinghall Street.*
Mr. Knightly *Hackney.*
Rand. Knipe *Fanchurch street.*

Jasper

[K.]

Jasper	Kawes *Thames street* near *Alhallows*.
John	Kouse *Pauls Wharf*.
John	Kroger *Waping, Execution-Dock, in the East-walk Exchange*.

[*L.*]

Tho.	Lackstone	*Leadenhall Street.*
Mr.	Lagley	*Threadneedle Street.*
Mr.	Lambeth	*Creed Church Lane.*
John	Lamb	*Cullam Street.*
Mr.	Lamb	*Bell-Alley Coleman-street.*
Ezek.	Lampaine	*Dove-Court Swithins Lane.*
John	Langham	*Leadenhall Street.*
John	Langley	*Great Saint Hellens.*
Mr.	Lang	*Lymestreet.*
Mr.	Langford	*ditto.*
Mr.	Langton	*Bankside.*
Mr.	Lanvey	*Dukes Place.*
John	Langworth	*Basinghall str. Blackwelhall Factor.*

Sam.

[*L.*]

Sam.	Lamott	*Wheatsheaf-Alley Thames Street.*
George	Lawrence	*Mark lane.*
Sir John	Lawrence	*Great Saint Hellens.*
John & Pet.	Lawrence	*Queenstreet.*
Jam.	Lawrey	*Crooked lane.*
Gawyn	Lawrey	*Three Kings Court Lombard street.*
Steph.	Lawes	*Beerbinder lane.*
Mr.	Lawefwood	*Tower street.*
John	Law	*Bankside.*
John	Lavero	*Lymestreet.*
Mr.	Lasher	*Little Tower hill.*
Mr.	Layta	*Aldermanbury.*
Mr.	Leigh	in *Cullam street*, in *Comp. with* Thomas.
Mr.	Leekins	*Newington Town.*
Jos.	Lee	*Throgmorton street.*
Ralph	Lee	*Threadneedle street.*
Mr.	Lee	*George Yard Lombard Street.*
Godfrey	Lee	*Coleman Street.*

John

[*L.*]

Ald. John Lane, *in St. Lawrence-lane.*
Gerard Langerman, *Burchin-lane.*
John Legendre *Nags-head Court Gracechurch street at Mr.* Heybert.
John Legg *London Wall.*
Mr. Legg *Coleman street.*
Mr. Legole *Basinghall street.*
Isaac Legay *Finsbury.*
David Legrill *Beerbinder lane.*
John Lemkuell *Crooked lane.*
Benj. Lenud, *Bucklersbury.*
Hertag. Lenton *Broadstreet near London-wall.*
Mr. Lepiner *Southwark.*
Sir Jo. Lethulier *Mark lane.*
Samuel ⎫
Will & ⎬ Lethulier, *Broadstreet.*
Abra. ⎭
Chisto. Lethulier *Turn-wheel-lane.*
Mr. Leuthalier *Bush lane.*
Nath. Letton *Fanchurch-street.*
John Letton *Turn-wheel-lane.*

[*L.*]

Steph.	Lewis, *Fan-Church-ſtreet.*
Thomas	Lewis, *little St. Hellens.*
John	Lewis, *St. Mary Hill.*
John	Lewis, *Poultrey.*
Sam.	Lewin *Barnaby-ſtreet.*
Charles	Lequein, *Crown Court in Spittle-fields.*
George	Leygo, *the Bridge.*
Robert	Liddell, *Cornhill.*
Mr.	Lightfoot, *Abchurch-lane.*
James	Lile, *St. Mary Hill.*
Mr.	Lille, *Dowgate.*
Roger	Lillington, *Ironmonger-lane.*
Humph.	Linton, *Broadſtreet.*
James	Littleton, *Berry-ſtreet.*
Thomas	Little, *Thames-ſtreet.*
Mr.	Littlepage *Clements-lane.*
Mr.	Littlepage, *Abchurch-lane.*
Mr.	Lock *St. Bartholmew Cloſe.*
Samuel	Lock, *Rood-lane.*
Mr.	Lock, *Tower-ſtreet.*
Mr.	Lock, *Goodmans-fields.*

Mr.

[*L.*]

Mr.	Lodwick,	*Fan-Church-street.*
Henry	Lombery,	*Cheapside at the Kings Arms.*
Mr.	Longbottom,	*Basinghall-street, Blackwell-hall-Factor.*
Timothy	Lemotuux,	*in Bow lane.*
Henry	Loo,	*London-wall.*
William	Lob,	*Tower-street.*
Mr.	Lofe,	*Bank-side.*
Henry	Loads	*St. Mary-hill.*
Sir Will.	Loder,	*Mark-lane.*
Jacob	Luce,	*Fan-Church-street.*
Michael	Luce,	*Dukes-Place.*
Mr.	Ludlow,	*Bow-lane.*
Nath.	Lodington,	*Aldermanbury.*
James	Lordell	*Fish-street-hill by the Monument.*
John	Lorimore,	*Rood-lane.*
John	Lord,	*Austin-Fryers, at Mr. Gar Vanvythusten.*
Mr.	Lorcaine	*Queen-street.*
John	Longent	*Fan-Church-str.*

[*L.*]

Ald. Love, *St. Mary Ax.*
Moſe Lowman, *Fan-Church-street.*
John Lloyd, *Martins-lane.*

[M.]

MR. Mace, *Lyme-street.*
David Malvin *St. Dunstans hill.*
Mr. Man, *Lyme-street.*
Mr. Mansfield, *Queen-street.*
Samuel Mansfield, *Gravelane. Hounds-ditch.*
John Maning, *Loathburry.*
Ralph Maning *and* Hide, *Coleman-street.*
Joseph Martin, *Rood-lane.*
Jasper Martin, *Mark-lane.*
John Martin, *Garlick-hill.*
Mr. Martin, *Hatton-Garden.*
John Martin, *Broad-street.*
Mr. Mart, Hatton-Garden.
Mr. Marandew, *Berry-street.*

[*M.*]

Mead.	Marvill, *Threadneedle-street.*
Samuel	Marvill, *Seething-lane.*
Mr.	Marriot, *Threadneedle-street.*
Mr.	Marsh, *St. Mary-Ax.*
Mr,	Marsh, *Trinity-lane.*
Mr.	Marsh, *Finsbury.*
Rich.	Marsh, *Shore-ditch.*
Mr.	Marsh, *Lambeth.*
George	Marwood, *Lawr. Pount. lane.*
Briant	Marshall *at a Packer's in Mincin-lane.*
John	Marshall, *Barnaby-street.*
Mr.	Marshall, *Montague-Close Southwark.*
Widd.	Marke, *Fan-Church-street.*
Mr.	Markum, *Wine-Office-Court, Fleet-street.*
John	Marvin, *Crutchet-fryars.*
The	*Widdow of* Lawr. Martell *in Fanchurch street.*
James	Marthwaite, *Leaden-hall-street.*

Robert

[*M.*]

Robert Masters, *Crutchet-Fryers.*
Robert Masters, *Leaden-hall-str.*
John Mascal, *Throgmorton-street.*
Robert Mason, *Nicholas-lane.*
Nath. Mason, *Bell-Alley Coleman-street.*
Mr. Mason, *Iron-monger-lane, Blackwel-hall Factor.*
John Matthews, *St. Mary-hill.*
Sir John Matthews, *in Fan-Church-street, at a Packers near Cullam-street.*
George Matson, *lodger at an Upholsterer's, Cornhill.*
Mr. Matthews, *Bow-lane.*
William Matthews, *Scotyard in Bush-lane.*
Richard Matthews, *Basing-hall-street, Blackwell-hall-Factor.*
John Mead, *Great St. Hellens.*
William Mead *Fan-Church-street.*
Robert Matthews, *in Crutchet-Fryers.*

[*M.*]

Nicholas Mead, *at a Confectioners, in Leadenhall street, near Lyme street.*
John Mead, *Tower-hill.*
John Mear, *Tower Royal.*
Henry Meas, *Berry-street.*
William Metcalf, *at the Cross-keys, Camomile-street.*
Robert Melish, *Philpot-lane.*
Mr. Mepot, *Throgmorton-street.*
John Morden, *Bishopsgate-street.*
Mr. Merreday, *Cateaton-street.*
Mr. Mereton, *King-street.*
Thomas Merry and Comp. *Garlick hill.*
Daniel Mercer, *Bartholomew-lane.*
Samuel Merrel, *Seething-lane.*
John Merlin, *Broad-street.*
Mr. Mevill *near Fishmongers Hall, Thames-street.*
Mr. Merat, *Grace-Church-str.*
Mr. Megoll, *Gravel-lane, Houndsditch.*
Mark Maubart, *Throgmorton-street, New Court.*

Samuel,

[*M.*]

Samuel⎫
and   ⎬ Michael, *Poultrey.*
Charles⎭

Mr.   Michael, *the Bridge.*
Bernard   Michael, *Clements - lane, Nags-head Court.*
Richard   Middleton, *Crutchet-fryers.*
Mr.   Middleton, *Coleman-street.*
Francis   Miller, *Throgmorton-street.*
Mr.   Miller, *Lyme-street.*
William   Miles, *Lombard-street* at Tho. White's.
Edward   Miles, *Bush-lane.*
Francis   Millington, *Lawr. Pount. lane.*
Mr.   Mitton, *in Aldermanbury.*
John   Mitford, *Fan-Church-str.*
Robert   Mitford, *Tenter - Alley, More-fields.*
Anthony   Mingay, *Swithins - lane, near Lombard-street.*
John   Miggot, *Threadneedle-str.*
Mark   Mortimore, *Tower-hill.*
Mr.   Moria, *great St. Hellens.*

John

[*M.*]

John Morgan, *Lodger, at Mr.* Hopegoods, *Throgmorton-street.*
Peter Moreman, *at a Packers in Mincin-lane.*
Samuel Morse, *Austin-Fryers.*
Edward Morse, *Token-house-yard at Mr.* Drapers.
William Morse *ditto.*
John Moris, *Austin-Fryers.*
Humph. Moris, *Broad-street.*
Richard Moris, *Cateaten-street.*
Mr. Morto, *Ropemakers-Alley.*
Thomas Morgan, *Aldermanbury.*
Simon Morse, *Cheapside.*
Nicholas Moysie, *Pancras-lane.*
Moses Mocate, *Camomile-street.*
Mr. Montey, *great St. Hellens.*
Mr. Montey, *Jewen-street.*
Richard Monniel, *Princess-street.*
Peter Montage, *Austin-Fryers.*
Stephen Montage, *Winchester-street.*
Mr. Monuty, *Leaden-hall-str.*

Robert

[M.]

Robert	Monteth,	*at a Packers Lawr. Pount.-lane.*
Sir John	Moore,	*Mincin-lane.*
George	Moore,	*Minories.*
Henry	Moody,	*Colchester-street.*
Abra.	Moone,	*Great St. Hellens, Comp. with Chamberlain.*
Fred.	Mooles,	*Angel - Court Throgmorton-street.*
Peter	Mody,	*Walbrook, the sign of the Golden-key.*
Charles	Muddeford,	*Fan - Church street.*
Abra.	Mumma,	*Crutchet-Fryers.*
Mr.	Muson,	*Barnaby-street.*
Mr.	Muce,	*Fan-Church-street.*
Sam.	Moyer,	*Walbrook.*
Mr.	Moyer,	*Rope-makers-Alley.*

[N.]

Edward Neal, *Poultrey.*
Sir Godard Nelthorpe, *Clarkenwell.*
James Nelthorpe, *Charterhouse Yard.*
John Nelson, *Cannon-street.*
Captain Needum, *Aldermanbury.*
Mr. Nunsan, *Rosemary-lane.*
Benj. Newland, *Mark-lane.*
Samuel Newton, *Crown - Court, Grace-Church-street.*
John Newton, *Crutchet-Fryers.*
John Newton, *Mile-end-Town.*
August. Newball, *Grub-street.*
John Nichols, *Tower-hill.*
Phil. Nichols, *ditto.*
John Nichols, *Mincin-lane.*
Daniel Nichols, *Ironmonger-lane.*
Richard Nichols, *Rosemary-lane.*
Edward Nichols, *Broad-street.*
Humph. Nicholson, *Mile-end-green.*
Jeff.

[N.]

Jeff.	Nightingall, *Clements-lane.*
Lawr.	Nigi, *Walbrook, Bonds Court.*
Henry	Norton, *ditto.*
Mr.	Norton, *Catcaten-street.*
Daniel	Norton, *Cornhill.*
Heneage	Norton, *at Mr.* Willoughby *Throgmorton-street.*
Mr.	Norington, *Grace-Church-street.*
Mr.	Norder, *the Horse-Ferry, Westminster.*
James	Nunns, *near Dukes-Place.*
William	Nutt, *Gun-yard Hounds-ditch.*
Mr.	Nuport, *Cateaten-street, Blackwell-hall, Factor.*

[O.]

MR.	Oadick, *Austin-Fryers.*
Pet.	Oleverez, *Dukes-Place.*
Hermin	Olmius, *Bishopsgate without Angel-Alley.*
Robert	Oldworth, *Copt-hall-court, Throgmorton-street.*
Richard	Onslow, *Hatton-Garden.*
Thomas	Ondby, *Aldermanbury.*
Peter	Otgar, *St. Mary-hill.*
Justin and Abra.	Otgat at Ald. Dogget, *Lawrence Pount. hill.*
William	Otwood, *Lyme-street.*
Peter	Orgueld, *Peter-hill.*
Mr.	Orey, *Pudding-lane.*
Egbert	Outvarst, *Great St. Hellens.*
John	Osgood, *White-Hart Court, Grace-Church-street.*

Cornel.

[O.]

Cornel. Oswald, *Berry-street.*
Richard Owens, *Swan-Alley, Coleman street.*
Peter Oversheld, *St. Mary-Ax.*
Richard Overman, *Oxford Court Cannon-street.*
Mr. Oyles, *Basing-hall-street, Blackwell-hall, Factor.*
Richard Oakley, *in Coleman-street, Blackwell-hall, Factor.*

JOhn Page, *Bishopsgate-street.*
Mr. Pagetor, *Hogsdan.*
William Paggen, *St. Dunstan Hill.*
William Pain, *ditto.*
Mr. Painer, *Camomile Street.*
Abra. Palmentier, *in Goldsmith Street.*
Edward Palmer, *Nicholas Lane.*
William Palmer, *Bishopsgate without Angel Alley.*
Thomas Papillion, *Fan-Church-Str.*
Mr. Patts, *Fan-Church Street.*
Mr. Panier, *St. Mary-Ax.*
Mr. Panton, *Chiswell Street.*
Peter Paravicin, *Fanchurch str.*
Mr. Parker, *Buttolph-Lane.*
Robert Parker, *Fish-street Hill.*
Mr. Parker, *Throgmorton Street.*
Andrew Pancier, *in New Court Throgmorton street.*

Francis

[*P.*]

Francis Pargetor, *Mon - Yard Black Fryers.*
Lewis Paran, *Bell Alley, Coleman Street.*
Mr. Parret, *Stepney.*
Daniel Parret, *Lawrence Pount Hill.*
Mr. Parr, *little Moore Fields.*
Mr. Parsons, *Ironmonger Lane.*
Edward Parr, *Koxis Key.*
John Peatorson; *at a Packers in Basinghall Street.*
Sir John Peak *Grace-Church Street.*
William Peak, *Leadenhall Street.*
Benj. Peak, *Winchester Street.*
William Pocock, *Basinghall Street.*
Richard Peele, *Bankside.*
William Pennington *St. Mary-Ax.*
Isaac Pennington, *Well - Court, Queen Street.*
William Pendarvis, *Lyme Street.*
Richard Pendarvis, *Swithins Lane.*
Samuel Pen, *Without Algate.*
David Persore, *Dukes-Place.*

[*P.*]

Movill and Lopes	Perrera, *Dukes-Place.*
William	Petters, *Throgmorton Str.*
Mr.	Pethouse, *Love Lane.*
Mr.	Peps, *Threadneedle Street.*
Thomas	Phillips, *Martins Lane.*
Mr.	Phillips, *Bankside.*
Mr.	Phillips, *Com. with Browne Lombard Street.*
Sir Rich.	Pickett, *Loathbury.*
Mr.	Pickett, *Berry Street.*
Mr.	Pickett, *Colledge Hill.*
Mr.	Pickett, *Fishstreet Hill at an Apothecary's.*
James	Pickering, *and Comp. Nicholas Lane for Ordnary.*
Thomas	Pilkington *Bush Lane Scot Yard.*
William	Pistorius, *at Mr. Whitehead Packer in Broad-Street.*
Mr.	Pinchback *in Ironmonger Lane.*
Phillip	Pim, *Mincin Lane.*

Stephen

[*P.*]

Stephen Pitts, *St. Dunstan Hill.*
Mr. Pitts, *the Bridge.*
William Plymton *London Wall Cross-keys Court.*
Mr. Playfoot, *Old Jury Blackwelhall Factor.*
Mr. Polixfield, *Walbrook.*
Thomas Polter, *Dukes-Place.*
Henry Polstead, *Bednal-Green.*
Mr. Ponia, *New Court Throgmorton Street.*
Mr. Pompillion, *Newsmans Yard Cornhill.*
Mr. Ponder, *Tower Street.*
James Pope, *Abchurch Lane.*
Alexand. Pope, *Broadstreet.*
Joseph Pope, *Redriff.*
Daniel Portaine, *Berry Street.*
William Portington, *Swithins lane.*
Mr. Pordage, *Lawr. Pountney Lane.*
John Pordage, *Cheapside, at the Swan and Harp.*
Josia Potter, *Loathbury.*
Mr. Potter, *Old Jury.*

[P.]

George Potts, *Tower Street.*
Henry Pottinger, *Bankside.*
William Powell, *Abchurch Lane.*
Mr. Powell, *the Bridge.*
William Poulden, *Gravill Lane, Hounds-ditch.*
William Poynes, *Throgmorton Str.*
Thomas Poynes, *Broad Street.*
Mr. Prawing, *Oxford Court, Cannon Street.*
Mr. Predox, *Michael Lane.*
John Prestwood, *Coleman Street.*
Captain Preston, *Mile-end-Green.*
Paul Priaulx, *Finsberry.*
Jos. Prickman, *Fanchurch Str-*
Mr. Prickmez, *St. Mary-Ax.*
John Price, *Three King Court, Lombard Street.*
William Priscott, *Angel Court, Throgmorton Street.*
Edward Puckridge, *Broad Street.*
Robert Puckell, *Thames Street near Gally-key.*
Thomas Puckle, *Austin-Fryers.*
Samuel Putt *Beerbinder Lane.*

Mr

[*R.*]

Mr.   Putick, *Berry Street.*
John   Pym, *Winchester Street.*
David   Prole, *Basinghall Street, Blackwell Hall Factor.*
Sir Will. Prayward, *at Carpenters Hall London-wall.*

[*R.*]

FRancis Rainsford, *Bow lane.*
    John Raimez, *Mincin lane.*
James   Ralphson, *Chequer Yard, Dowgate.*
Matthew   Randall, *Chain Alley.*
Mr.   Randall, *Fanchurch Street.*
Matthew   Randall, *Throgmorton Str.*
Edward   Randall, *Queen Street.*
Mr.   Randfosse, *great S. Hellens.*
Mr.   Ranalson, *Martins lane.*
Francis   Rape, *at a Confectioners in Walbrook.*
Mr.   Ratliff, *Fishstreet Hill.*

[*R.*]

George Ravencroft, *Westminster, Turkey Walk Exchange.*
John Rawlins, *Cloapton Hackney.*
John Rayner, *Leadenhall street.*
John Rayner, *Clements lane.*
Mr. Rayledge, *Devonshire-House.*
Mr. Reanals, *Basinghall street, Blackwel Hall Factor.*
Thomas Rea, *Princess Street.*
Mr. Reeves, *Great St. Hellens.*
Jos. Reeves, *Barnarby Street.*
John Reede, *Aldermanbury.*
Stephen Reade, *Leadenhall Street.*
Thomas Reeve, *Cornhill, lodger at an Upholsterers.*
William Regoat, *Gravil lane, Hounds-ditch.*
Arthur Remington, *Broad Street.*
Peter Renew, *Philpot lane.*
Theoph. Revell, *Thames Street near Billingsgate.*
John Richardson, *Water lane.*
Rand. Richardson, *near Fishmongers Hall.*

Edward

[R.]

Edward Richbell, *Berry Street.*
Mr. Richmond, *Harp lane.*
John Riches, *Lawr. Pount. lane.*
Captain Rich, *Bankſide.*
Henry Ricardus, *at Ald.* Jeffery's *Berry Street.*
Mr. Richards, *without New-gate.*
Mr. Ridley, *Grubſtreet.*
William Robards, *Leadenhall ſtreet.*
Richard Robards, *without Biſhops-gate.*
Gab. Robards, *London - Wall, Carpenters Hall.*
Gar. Robards, *White Hart Court, Grace Church ſtr.*
Thomas Robards, *George Yard, Lombard Street.*
Mr. Robards, *Crooked lane.*
Mr. Robards. *Berry Street.*
Lenc. Robinſon, *and Comp. Nicholas's lane.*
Andrew Robinſon, *Three Kings Court: Lombard Street.*
William Robinſon, *Mark lane.*

G 4 Mr.

[R.]

Mr.	Robinſon, *Crooked lane.*
George	Robins, *ditto.*
Mr.	Robulus, *Berry Street.*
Gomez	Rodrigues, *ditto.*
Nicholas	Roo, *Leadenhall Street.*
Richard	Roo, *White Hart Court Grace Church Street.*
Mr.	Roo, *Corbit Court Grace Church Street.*
Rand.	Roper, *near the Armitage.*
Jos.	Rookſby, *Mincin lane.*
Mr.	Rookſby ⎱ *Stepney.*
Mr.	Rookſby ⎰
John	Rowland, *Winchester ſtreet.*
Nicholas	Rowles, *Threadneedle ſtr.*
Timothy	Royly, *Dowgate.*
John	Royly, *Soper lane.*
Samuel	Royſton, *Bucklers Berry.*
Jeremy	Royſton, *Poultrey.*
Edward	Rudge, *St. Mary-Ax.*
Mr.	Rudge, *Redriff.*
Richard	Ruſſell, *Buſh lane, Scot yard.*
Mr.	Ruſſell *by the Bridge.*
Mr.	Rucket, *Minories.*

[S.]

Mr. Sadler, *Mugwell Street.*
Mr. John Sadler, *Walbrook.*
Samuel Sale, *in Lymestreet Comp. with Scopin.*
Henry Salter, *Fanchurch street.*
Mr. Salter, *in Princes street.*
Richard Sallaway, *Oxford Court in Cannon street.*
John Sallaway, *at Mr. Cockrams Swithins lane.*
Samuel Sambrook, *Tower street.*
William Sambrook, *Queen street.*
Mr. Samuel, *Dukes-Place.*
Edward Sanders, *Thomas Apostles.*
John Sanders, *Throgmorton str.*
Philip Sanderson, *in St. Lowrence lane.*
Edward Sanders, *Buttolf lane.*
Mr. Sanders, *Thames street.*
Edward Sanders, *Newington Green.*
Henry Sanders, *Broad street.*
Mr.

[S.]

Mr.	Sanders, *Bucklers Berry*.
John	Sanford, *Basinghall street*.
Mr.	Sands, *Beerbinder lane*.
Mr.	Saneeis, *Talbot Court Grace Church street*.
Clem.	Sawyer, *little Trinity lane*.
John	Sawyer, *Ivy-lane*.
Abra.	Sayon *at Mr.* Stubbs *in Swithins lane*.
Lucas	Scantes, *Lyme-street*.
Mr.	Scanly, *the Bridge*.
William	Scarlet, *Tower street at a Drapers*.
Mr.	Scarlet, *Newington Green*.
Edward	Scuyt, *Loathybury at the Bear and Fountain*.
John	Scopen *and Comp. Lyme-street*.
William	Scoing, *Lawr. Pount. lane*.
Richard	Scot *Basinghall street*.
Mr.	Scot, *London-wall Blackwel Hall Factor*.
John	Serape, *Loathbury*.
Daniel	Scoken, *Threadneedle str*.
Mr.	Scowell, *Buttolph lane*.

Edward

[S.]

Edward	Seaman, *Thames street.*
Michael	Sederis, *Mark lane.*
Peter	Sedgwick, *in Martins lane.*
Obad.	Sedgwick, *Fanchurch str.*
Mr.	Sedgwick, *Beerbinder lane.*
Mr.	Sedgwick, *Swithins lane.*
Mr.	Seneris, *little Eastchip.*
Joseph	Serjeant, *St. John street, Irish-Walk Exchange.*
Arnold	Sertillion, *Fanchurch street.*
Arth.	Sexagomes, *Minories.*
Mr.	Shaw, *St. Dunstans Hill.*
John	Shelden, *Cannon street.*
John	Shelden *in Dukes - Place near the Church.*
William	Shelden, *the Bridge.*
Basal and Edmond	Sherman, *Tower Hill.*
William	Sherrington, *Bishopsgate street.*
Henry	Sheeth, *Aldermanbury.*
Samuel	Shepherd, *Michaels lane.*
Mr.	Shepherd, *Bucklersbury.*

John

[S.]

John Shepherd, *White Hart Court Grace Church str.*
Thomas Shepherd, *Abchurch lane.*
Mr. Sherbrook, *Company, with Mr. Clark in Cheapside.*
William Sherbrook, *St. Hellens.*
Sir John Shorter, *Bankside.*
James Sherlock, *at Queen Hive.*
Charles Shorter, *ditto.*
William Short, *Ditto.*
Mr. Shieres, *Crutchet Fryers.*
Mr. Shieres, *Ratliff Cross.*
Mr. Shilgrove, *Buttolph lane.*
William Shipman *Tower Hill.*
Mr. Sigues, *Goodmans Fields.*
William Sikes, *lodger at a Packers in Swithins lane.*
Edward Silvester *Thames street.*
Mr. Silvester *Cammile street.*
Mr. Silgrove, *Love lane.*
Mr. Silver, *Minories.*
Mr. Silver *Camomile-street.*
George and Robert } Sitwell, *Leadenhall str.*

Thomas

[S.]

Thomas	Symons, *Cateaton street.*
Edward	Symons, *Masons Alley in Cornhill.*
Michael	Sivex, *Mark lane.*
Daniel	Skinner, *Crutchet Fryers.*
Benj.	Skutt, *Great St. Hellens.*
John	Skinner, *Austin Fryers.*
Daniel	Skinner, *Barthol. lane.*
Mr.	Skinner, *Camberry House at Islington.*
Mr.	Skinner, *Ironmonger lane.*
Nath.	Skinner, *Kings Arms Yard Coleman street.*
Mr.	Skinner *in Cateaton street.* [sic.]
Richard	Slinger, *Philpot lane.*
Par.	Slater, *Basinghall street Blackwelhall-Factor.*
Benj.	Smart, *Broad street.*
Mr.	Smith *in Grubstreet.*
Sir Jam.	Smith, *Kings Arms Yard Coleman street.*
John	Smith *Camomile street.*
Nicholas and John	Smith, *Little St. Hellens.*

Nath.

[S.]

Nath. Smith, *Woodstreet, at an Apothecary's.*
John Smith *Cheapside.*
John Smith *Walbrook.*
Ald. Smith *Clarkenwell Green.*
Mr. Smith *ditto.*
Mr. Smith *ditto.*
Mr. Smith *Grubstreet.*
Mr. Smith *Water side near Billingsgate.*
Thomas Smith *backside the Exchange at a Packer's.*
Ald. Smith, *Bankside.*
Thomas Smith *Bankside at a Pack.*
William Smith *Bunhill.*
Mr. Smith, *Peter's Alley Cornh.*
James Smith *Clink street.*
John Smith *Mark lane.*
George Snell *Lawr. Pount. Hill.*
John Snelling *Tuly street.*
Mr. Snow *Shadwell.*
William Somers *Aldermary Church Yard.*
Mr. Southwell *Crutchet Fryers.*
Samuel Southton *Broad street.*

John

[S.]

John	South *George Yard Lombard street.*
Mr.	Southerby *Hackney.*
Peter	Southwick *Coleman street.*
Mr.	Spicer *Abchurch lane.*
Mr.	Spicer *Goodmans Fields.*
Mr.	Spencer *Minories.*
Mr.	Spencer *Newington Green.*
Peter	Split *Armitage Wapping.*
Henry	Spencer *Mark lane.*
Sir Tho.	Stamp *Basinghall street.*
George	Stanpel *a Stationer near the Exchange.*
Mr.	Standley, *St. Dunstans hill.*
Will,	Stavendish *Thames street.*
Mr.	Stacy *Pickle Herring.*
Mr.	Stacy *Thames street near Billingsgate.*
Isa.	Stackman *Broad street.*
Roger	Stackhard *Coleman street.*
Mr.	Stenenis *Berry street.*
Mr.	Steneque *Threadneedle str.*
Farly	Stephenson *at Billingsgate every morning.*
Mr.	Stevenson *Threadn. street.*
Mr.	Stevenson *Bishopsgate str.*

Richard [sic.]

[S.]

Thomas Stevenson *Old Fish-street.*
Richard Steele *Nags-head Court in Grace Church Street.*
Mr. Stenenis *Hogsdon.*
Mr. Steres *Tuly street.*
William Stiles *Shadwell.*
Mr. Stipkins *Pauls Wharf.*
Samuel Storey *Sice lane.*
John Storey *Bow Church Yard.*
John Story *Leadenhall street at a Packer's.*
Roger Stockhard *Coleman street.*
Mr. Stonnier *Durham Yard.*
Jer. Stone *Nich. lane.*
George Strinyard *Crutchet Fryers.*
Mr. Streete *Mark lane.*
Mr. Strood *Lawr. Pount. lane.*
Hugh Strood *Pudding lane.*
William Strude *at Mr. Atterberry Throgmorton street.*
Nath. Strange *Swithins lane at a Packer's.*
Mr. Stronge *Queen street.*
Mr. Stracey *Grace Church str.*

Henry

[S.]

Henry	Stroud *Lawr. Pount. lane.*
Anthony	Sturt *Minories.*
Mr.	Sturt *Throgmorton street.*
John	Stubbs *St. Swithins lane.*
Thomas	Stubbings *Cloak lane.*
Isaac & Jacob	Swares *Dukes-Place.*
Mr.	Swanham *St. Katherines.*
Samuel	Swinock, *Fanchurch street. Pye Alley.*
John	Swinton *Water-lane.*
Richard	Swithins *Lawr. Pount. Hill.*
Mr.	Swift *Welstreet Hackney.*
Mr.	Squib *Palace Yard West-minster.*
Bar.	Scirps *at Mr. Nelmes Packer in Beerbinder lane.*

[T.]

[T.]

James Tawden *St. Martins lane.*
John Tanner *Berry street.*
Mr. Tares *Dukes-Place.*
John Taylor *Basinghall street Blackwelhall Factor.*
John Taylor *Talbot Court Grace Church street.*
John Taylor *Budg Row.*
Mr. Taylor *Throgmorton str.*
Mr. Taylor *Newington Butts.*
Mr. Taylor *Wildstreet.*
John Taylor *Mile-end Green.*
James Taylor *Fleetstreet Peter-borough Court.*
Mr. Tedway *Distaff lane.*
James Therey *Fanchurch street.*
Mr. Terrenis, *Watling street.*
Mr. Terick *Kingsland.*
Isaac Tellis *Berry street.* Ald.

[T.]

Ald.	Tinch *Fanchurch street.*
Walter	Thimbleton *Bednal Green Irish Walk.*
Mr.	Thinn *Lawr. Pount. lane.*
Isaac	Testard *Throgmorton str.*
William	Throgmorton *Trinity lane.*
Sir Will.	Thompson *Lyme street.*
Major	Thompson *Newington.*
Francis	Thompson *Tower Hill.*
Kategen	Thomas *Bankside.*
William	Thomas *Cullam street.*
William	Thomas *Basinghall street Blackwelhall Factor.*
Christ.	Tomlinson *Martins Lane.*
Coll.	Thornborow *Mincin lane.*
Mr.	Thornwell *Lyme street.*
Robert	Thornton *ditto.*
Benj.	Thorowgood *Cornhill.*
Robert	Thorner *at Mr.* Leigh *Finsbury.*
Mr.	Thursby, *Bishopsg. without.*
William	Tichburn *Lawr. Pount. lane.*
Edward	Tidcombe *Coleman street.*
Richard	Tilden *Tower street.*

[T.]

Richard   Tilden *White Chappel.*
Mr.   Tilsoard *Chiswell street.*
Abra.   Tilard *Finsbury.*
Jos.   Tillingson *Kings Arms Yard Coleman street.*
Mr.   Tyson *Coleman street Blackwelhall Factor.*
Mr.   Tinch *Newington Green.*
Mr.   Tinch *St. Mary-Ax.*
Walt.   Tindall *Bunhill.*
Francis   Tierrens *St. Swithins lane.*
Mr.   Tolson *Cateaton street.*
Mr.   Tomliz *Bow Church Yard.*
George   Toriano *Nicholas lane.*
Ald. Fran.   Townely *Mincin lane.*
John   Townsend *Broad street.*
Robert   Townsend *Lawr. Pount. lane.*
Mr.   Townsend *Fishstreet Hill.*
Edward   Towes *Great St. Hellens.*
Benj.   Took *Loathbury.*
Mr.   Trannell *Tower Hill.*
Charles   Trinquand *Mark lane.*
George   Trinchard *Billiter lane.*
Mr.   Trenacker *Clopton Hackney.*
Theod.

[T.]

Theod. Trotle *near Fishmongers Hall Thames street.*
Mr. Tronantle *Bankside.*
Anthony Tretheuie *Portugal Row.*
Pier. Trott *Vine Court Bishopsgate without.*
Mr. Treres *St. Olives street Southwork.*
Mr. Tut *Berry street.*
Rignal Tucker *Rood lane.*
Sam. Tucker *Martins lane.*
John Tudman *Throgmorton str.*
Sir Hen. Tulce *Loathbury.*
Mr. Turpin *Throgmorton street.*
Mr. Turnel *Billiter lane.*
John Turner *Suffolk lane.*
Thomas Tuson *in Swithins lane.*
Thomas Twisden *Throgmorton str.*
Thomas Twisden *little Morefields.*
Francis Tyson *Philpot lane.*
Richard Torner *lodger at Mr. Edw. Wats in Mark lane.*

[V.]

Mr.	Vallentine	*Basinghall str. Blackwelhall Factor.*
Jasper	Vanderbrusten	*Thames str.*
Jo. Bapt.	Vanderhoeven	*Seething lane.*
Mr.	Vanderhou	*ditto.*
Phil. and Sebasta }	Vanbrewsigham	*Philpot lane.*
Christians	Vanbreda Samuel,	*Fan-Church street.*
Mr.	Vandamlyt	*Camomile str.*
George and William }	Vanham	*great S. Hellens.*
Ger.	Vanuythuyson	*Austin Fr.*
Mr.	Van Morris	*ditto.*
Daniel	Van Milder	*Throgmorton street.*
Peter	Vanden	*Anchor Lyme str.*
Widd.	Vandermarsh	*ditto.*

Peter

[V.]

Peter	Vandermarſh	*Martins lane.*
Peter	Vandebob	*Lawr. Pount. lane.*
William	Vandenbergh	*ditto.*
Peter	Vanderbuſten	*Alhallows Thames ſtreet.*
John	Vannerſon	*Kings Arms Yard Coleman ſtreet.*
Peter	Vandeput	*Baſinghall ſtr.*
John	Vanhack	*Abchurch lane.*
Mr.	Vannet	*Bucklers Berry.*
Mr.	Van Diuer	*Lawr. Pount. lane.*
Mr.	Van Bliſſe	*Wapping.*
Nicholas	Van Milder	*ditto.*
Daniel	Van Pray	*Clink ſtreet Mary-gold ſtairs Southw.*
John	Van Wachtendonek	*Leadenhall ſtreet.*
Law.	Vanham	*St. Katherines.*
Corn.	Vandures	*S. Swithins lane.*
Conſtan.	Vanetti	*Seething lane.*

[V.]

Peter	Van Cittert *at Mr.* John Martin Elkins *Lawrence Pount. lane.*
Francis	Van Acker *Abchurch lane.*
John	Van Laere *Paul's Church Yard near the School.*
Mr.	Vbetter *St. Mary Ax.*
Thomas and John	Varnon *Gravil lane Hounds-ditch.*
Mr.	Varnon *Hartichoak lane* [sic.] *Wapping.*
John	Varnon *Cherry-tree Alley little Morefields.*
John	Varnon *Coleman street.*
Thomas	Verbeck *Broad street.*
Calib	Veren *Pickled Herring.*
William	Veager *Bishopsg. without in White Hart Yard.*
Mr.	Vine *Armitage.*
Isaac	Vink *Austin Fryers.*
Peter	Vertirini *Mark lane.*
Mr.	Villeway *Montague Court Southwork.*
Mr.	Visher *St. Mary Hill.*

Mr.

[V.]

Mr. Vespreet *and* Vanden-brook *Lyme street.*
Cornel. Van Beselor Walter *in Crooked lane.*

[U.]

Henry Upton *Dukes-Place.*
Hugh Upton *ditto.*
Mr. Upton *Newington Town.*
Gilb. Upton *Cloak lane.*
Mr. Unis *Dukes-Place.*
Thomas Vernon *in Coleman street.*

[W.]

Tho. Wade *Sheerbon lane.*
Mr. Wade *Tower Hill.*
Henry Wade *Mincin lane comp. with Burkin.*
Matthew Walker *Throgmorton str.*

James.

[W.]

James Wallis *Fanchurch street.*
Ald. Waldow *Cheapside.*
Mr. Waldo *Spittle-fields.*
Anthony Wallinger *Oxford Court Cannon street.*
Abra. and John } Walwin *Lawr. Pount. hill.*
Sir Pat. Ward *Lawr. Pount. Hill.*
Mr. Ward *little Moor fields.*
Mr. Ward *Ironmonger lane.*
James Ward *Kings Arms Yard Coleman street.*
James Ward *Oxford Court Cannon street.*
Sir Will. Warren *Wapping.*
William Warren *Fanchurch street.*
Nicholas Warren *Lyme street.*
Mr. Warren *Gun Yard.*
Henry Warren *Old Jury.*
Mr. Warren *Old Jury Black-welhall Factor.*
William Warr *Seething lane.*
Mr. Wardner *Leaden Hall street.*

William

[W.]

William Warle *Fishstreet Hill.*
Edmond Warner *Throgmorton str.*
Mr. Warner *Angel Court S. Martins le Grand.*
Henry Warner *Colledge Hill.*
William Warner *Mincin lane.*
Samuel Wastall *Vine Court Spittle fields.*
Sir Geor. Waterman *Thames street.*
Ed. Watts *Mark lane.*
George Watts *Aldersgate street.*
John Watts *at Mr. Smarts in Broad street.*
Mich. Watts *Old Jury.*
Mr. Watkins *Lymestreet.*
Peter Watson *Aldermanbury Love lane.*
Mr. Watter *Colledge Hill.*
William Webb *Throgmorton street.*
Thomas Webb *ditto.*
Mr. Webb *London wall.*
James Welden *Princess street.*
Mr. Wells *little Moorefields.*
George Willington *and Comp. with* Alcock *Coleman street.*

Mat.

[IV.]

Mat.	Wentworth *Ironmonger lane Blackwelhall Fact.*
Mr.	Wentworth *Aldersgate str.*
Phil. and John	Werts *Crutchet Fryers.*
Ger.	Westcomb *great S. Hellens.*
Richard	Westcomb *Lyme street.*
Mr.	Westbrook *Aldermanbury.*
Mr.	Westhorne *Ironmonger lane.*
Oliver	Westland *Bishopsgate str. lodger at an Upholsterers.*
Nath.	Westland *Bankside.*
Mr.	West *Petty France Morefields.*
Abra.	Wesset *Bishopsgate street without Whitegate Alley.*
Ger.	Weymans *Thames street.*
Mr.	Weymanslet *Bankside.*
Mr.	Winise *Philpot lane.*
Mr.	Winbart *Mincin lane.*
Mr.	Whistler *Sheerbon lane.*
Mr.	Wilson *Old Jury Blackwelhall Factor.*

Mr.

[W.]

Mr.	Whatton and Wilcox *Cheapside.*
Thomas	Whitebread *Mark lane.*
John	Whithall *Philpot lane.*
Sir Steph. and Mr.	White *Kingsland Spanish Walk Exchange.*
William	White *Fanchurch street.*
Thomas	White *Minories Goodmans Yard.*
Mr.	Whitefield *Dukes-Place.*
John	Whitehead *Aldermanbury.*
William	Whitehead *Petty France.*
John	Whithead *Broad street.*
Mr.	Whiting *Coleman street Blackwelhall Factor.*
Mr.	Woolkins *in Basinghall str. Blackwelhall Factor.*
George	Woodford *Basinghall str. Blackwel hall Factor.*
Mr.	Woodward *Thames street.*
Jonath.	Woodhouse *ditto.*
William	Wood *Wapping.*
Mr.	Wood *in Basinghall str. Blackwelhall Factor.*
	Mr.

Mr.	Wood *Berry street.*
Mr.	Woodman *Wapping.*
Mr.	Woolhouse *St. Mary-Ax.*
Adam	Wooley *Bucklers Berry.*
Robert	Wooley *Mincin lane.*
Mr.	Woots *Cateaton street.*
John	Wolf *Little Moore fields.*
Mr.	Woodroft *Little St. Bartholomews.*
Mr.	Wordner *St. Mary-Ax.*
Mr.	Wosham *Broad street.*
Mr.	Wildy *Basinghall street Blackwell-hall Factor.*
Henry	Wild *near the Old Swan Thames street.*
Nicholas and Ralph	Wild *Billiter lane.*
George	Willoughby *Throgmorton street.*
Robert	Wilson *Little More-fields.*
Thomas	Wilson *Bishopsgate without.*
Mr.	Wilson *Broad street.*
Robert	Williamson *Turn-wheel lane.*

James

[*W.*]

James Williamson Lawr. Pount. lane.
John Wilmor Jewen street.
Humph. Willet Swithins lane.
William Willis and Gore Swan Alley Coleman street.
Mr. Willoughby Mark lane.
William Window Tower Hill.
Mr. Winhack Aldermanbury.
Mr. Wife Fanchurch street.
Thomas Wife and Lumbes Threadneedle street.
Mr. Winefield Buttolph lane.
Mr. Winch Shadwell.
Mr. Winash Armitage.
Benj. Wetcomb Coleman street
Mr. Wilcox Basinghall street Blackwelhall Factor.
Mr. Wright Water-lane.
Mr. Wright Bankside.
Jos. Wright Aldersgate street
Mr. Wright near St. Thomas Apostles.

[Y.]

[Y.]

Mr. Yates *the Bridge.*
Fran. Young *Mincin lane.*
Richard Young *Leadenhall street.*
James Young *Dukes-Place.*
Nath. Young *at the African House.*
Thomas Yoakly *Tower street in a Court near Mark lane.*
Thomas Yoakſly *in Cannon street near the Blew Bell.*

Hereunto is added an Addition of all the Goldsmiths that keep Runing Cashes.

A.

JOhn Addis *and Company at the Sun in Lumbard street.*

B.

JOhn Bolitho *and Mr. Wilson at the Golden Lion in Lumbard street.*
John Ballard *at the Unicorn Lumbard street.*
Job Bolton *at the Bolt and Tun in Lumbard Street.*
Richard Blanchard and Child } *at the Marygold in Fleetstreet.*
Thomas

C

Thomas Cook and Nicholas Cary } *at the Griffin in Exchange Alley.*
Mr. Cutbert *in Cheapside.*
Mr. Coggs *in the Strand at the Kings-head.*
Mr. Churchill *at the   in the Strand.*

D

CHar. Duncomb and Richard Kent } *at the Grashopper in Lumbard street.*

E

JOhn Ewing and Benj. Norington } *at the Angell and Crown in Lumbard str.*
Mr. East *at the   in the Strand.*

F

THomas Fowles *at the Black Lion in Fleetstreet.*

Joseph

H

Joseph and Nath. } Hornboy *at the Star in Lumbard street.*

H

JOhn Hind } *over against the Exchange in*
Thomas Carwood } *Cornhill.*

Benj. Hinton *at the Flower de Luce in Lumbard* street.

James Herriot *at the Naked Boy in Fleetstreet.*

James Hore *at the Golden Bottle in Cheapside.*

J

JAmes Johnson *at the Three Flower de Luces in Cheapside.*

K.

THo. Kilborne and Capill } *at the Kings Head in Lumbard street.*

L

Mr. Kenton *at the* Kings-Arms *in Fleetstreet.*

Mr. Ketch *at the* Black-Horse *in the Strand.*

L

Henry Lamb *at the Grapes in Lumbard street.*

James Lapley *at the Three Cocks Cheapside.*

M

John Mawson *and Comp. at the Golden Hind in Fleet str.*

N

Henry Nelthorpe *at the Rose in Lumbard street.*

P

Tho. Price *at the Goat in Lumbard street.*

Peter Percefull ⎫
and   ⎬ *at the Black Boy in Lumbard street.*
Stephen Evans ⎭

Thomas

R

Thomas Pardo *at the Golden Anchor in Lumbard street.*

R

THo. Rowe
and
Thomas Green } *at the George in Lumbard street.*

S.

HUmph. Stocks *at the Black-Horse in Lumbard str.*
John Sweetaple *at the Black-Moors-Head in Lumbard street.*
John Snell *at the Fox in Lum-street.*
Michael Schrimpshaw *at the Golden Lion in Fleetstreet.*
Richard Stayley *in Covent Garden.*

T

JOhn Temple
and
John Seale } *at the Three Tunns in Lumbard str.*
John Thursby *at the Ball in Lumbard street.*

I 3 Bar.

W

Bar. Turner and Samuel Tookie } *at the Fleece in Lumbard street.*

W

Major Joh. Wallis *at the Angell in Lumbard street.*

Peter Wade *at the Mearmaid in Lumbard street.*

Peter White and Churchill } *at the Plough in Lumbard street.*

Thomas White *at the Blew Anchor in Lumbard street.*

Thomas Williams *at the Crown in Lumbard street.*

Robert Ward and John Towneley } *at the Ram in Lumbard str.*

THo. Flowerdew *at* Rowl. Dee *in the Poultrey.*
Benj. Bathurft *St. Mary-Ax.*
Benj. Rigfath *Nicholas lane.*
Jafp. Chapman *Bafinghall ftr.*
Peter Vergrew *in New Court in Throgmortou ftreet.*
John Conine *in Salifbury Court.*
Auguft Allard *in Kings ftreet.*
Will. Faffet *Dutch Walk Exch.*
Ja. Caepell *at the Bee-hive in Watlin ftreet.*
George Cokp *near St. Dunftan's lodger at a Widdows.*
Hougo *and* John Lent *at a Packers St. Dunftan's Hill.*
John Burrow *in Bufh lane.*
Cap. Nunffan *at the Infur. Office.*
Edw. Blake *Tower ftreet.*
Nich. Lock *Batholomew Clofe.*
John Blake *St. Swithins lane at a Packer's.*
Will. Depeftor *Broad ftreet at the Surgeons Arms.*

John

John Edmonds *in Philpot lane.*
Edw. Wards *Basinghall street.*
James Eyton *Fish-street Hill.*
Warw. Yard *African-House.*
Samuel Burlingham and Comp. *in Angel Court in Lumbard street.*
Ralph Far *at Mile-end Green.*
Paul Alestry *in St. Martins lane.*
John Bruse *Fanchurch str.*
Mr. Brabant *in St. Swithins lane at a Packer's.*
Samuel Braborne *at his Brother Mr. Braborne in the Poultry.*
Simon Clark *in Love lane Aldermanbury.*
Adrian Van Schipcroot *in Muddiford Court Fanchurch str.*
John Morris *at Mr. Baker's Almary Church Yard.*
Stat. Ahearns *Lawr. Poult. Hill.*

CHISWICK PRESS:
REPRINTED BY WHITTINGHAM AND WILKINS,
TOOKS COURT, CHANCERY LANE.

www.ingramcontent.com/pod-product-compliance
Lightning Source LLC
Chambersburg PA
CBHW030346170426
43202CB00010B/1271